NEW HAVEN PUBLIC LIBRARY

DATE DUE

Paul Robeson

ENTERTAINER AND ACTIVIST

Muhammad Ali	Spike Lee
Maya Angelou	Malcolm X
Louis Armstrong	Bob Marley
Josephine Baker	Thurgood Marshall
George Washington Carver	Eddie Murphy
Ray Charles	Barack Obama
Johnnie Cochran	Jesse Owens
Bill Cosby	Rosa Parks
Frederick Douglass	Colin Powell
W.E.B. Du Bois	Condoleezza Rice
Jamie Foxx	Paul Robeson
Aretha Franklin	Chris Rock
Marcus Garvey	Al Sharpton
Savion Glover	Will Smith
Alex Haley	Clarence Thomas
Jimi Hendrix	Sojourner Truth
Gregory Hines	Harriet Tubman
Billie Holiday	Nat Turner
Langston Hughes	Madam C.J. Walker
Jesse Jackson	Booker T. Washington
Magic Johnson	Oprah Winfrey
Scott Joplin	Stevie Wonder
Coretta Scott King	Tiger Woods
Martin Luther King Jr.	

Paul Robeson

ENTERTAINER AND ACTIVIST

Louise Chipley Slavicek

CHELSEA HOUSE
An Infobase Learning Company

Paul Robeson

Copyright © 2011 by Infobase Learning

Chelsea House
An imprint of Infobase Learning
132 West 31st Street
New York, NY 10001

Library of Congress Cataloging-in-Publication Data

Slavicek, Louise Chipley, 1956–
Paul Robeson : entertainer and activist / by Louise Chipley Slavicek.
    p.   cm. — (Black Americans of achievement, legacy edition)
Includes bibliographical references and index.
ISBN 978-1-60413-843-6 (hardcover)
1. Robeson, Paul, 1898–1976—Juvenile literature. 2. African Americans—Biography—Juvenile literature. 3. Actors—United States—Biography—Juvenile literature. 4. Singers—United States—Biography—Juvenile literature. 5. Political activists—United States—Biography—Juvenile literature. I. Title. II. Series.
E185.97.R63S53 2011
791.092—dc22   [B]   2010026879

You can find Chelsea House on the World Wide Web at http://www.chelseahouse.com.

Text design by Keith Trego
Cover design by Keith Trego and Takeshi Takahashi
Composition by Keith Trego
Cover printed by Bang Printing, Brainerd, MN
Book printed and bound by Bang Printing, Brainerd, MN
Date printed: January 2011
Printed in the United States of America

10 9 8 7 6 5 4 3 2 1

This book is printed on acid-free paper.

All links and Web addresses were checked and verified to be correct at the time of publication. Because of the dynamic nature of the Web, some addresses and links may have changed since publication and may no longer be valid.

Contents

Peekskill, New York: September 4, 1949

On the afternoon of Sunday, September 4, 1949, some 15,000 concertgoers gathered at an abandoned golf course just outside of Peekskill, New York, about 40 miles (64 kilometers) north of New York City. They had come to hear performing artist and social activist Paul Robeson, arguably the most famous black person in the United States in 1949. A former college football star, Robeson became an internationally renowned stage and film actor and concert singer in the late 1920s. By the end of World War II in 1945, Robeson's many professional accomplishments included critically acclaimed performances in London and Broadway productions of William Shakespeare's *Othello, the Moor of Venice*; a string of hit records; and dozens of sold-out concerts in cities across Europe and North America. At the same time, Robeson was becoming just as well known for his controversial political views as tensions between the United States and its Communist archrival, the Soviet Union, intensified following the war.

"THE CHALLENGE MUST BE TAKEN UP"

While touring the Union of Soviet Socialist Republics (USSR) in the 1930s, Robeson became convinced that the Soviet leadership was sincerely devoted to the same social and political ideals that he held dearest. Among these were giving workers a greater share in the wealth their labor helped to create; ending colonial rule in Africa and throughout the world; and guaranteeing complete equality to people of all races, something that African Americans were still a long way from achieving. Robeson's outspoken praise for the Soviets during World War II raised few eyebrows in his homeland, since the United States and the Soviet Union were, along with Great Britain, wartime allies against the Axis Powers of Germany, Italy, and Japan. After the war, however, when the Soviet military takeover of Eastern Europe fueled U.S. fears regarding Russian ambitions in Europe and Communist subversion at home, Robeson's open admiration for the USSR no longer sat well with many Americans. Anti-Robeson sentiment skyrocketed in April 1949, when, on a visit to Paris, he declared that, should Russia and America go to war, black Americans could not be expected to fight against the USSR, which he believed was "the only nation in the world where racial discrimination is prohibited." Newspaper editorials across the United States accused Robeson of being a Communist and a traitor; when Robeson returned home that June, he found himself banned from most American concert halls and theaters, as well as from television and radio broadcasts.

After Robeson announced his plans to perform at a fundraising concert for the Civil Rights Congress, a left-leaning civil rights organization, in Peekskill, on August 27, 1949, local newspapers and veterans groups angrily objected, accusing the singer-activist of being unpatriotic and a Communist sympathizer. The concert had to be canceled at the last minute when a large group of rock-throwing protesters attacked the first concertgoers to arrive that afternoon. The protesters' attack on the racially mixed audience members had racist overtones, with the rioters shouting racial slurs and even burning a Ku Klux Klan–style cross. Robeson, though, was not about to be intimidated. The day after the canceled concert, he announced that the Peekskill event was rescheduled for September 4. Protection for Robeson was to be provided by several racially mixed left-leaning trade unions.

The September 4 concert went smoothly, with Robeson performing a selection of African-American spirituals and international folk songs before concluding with a stirring rendition of his signature song, "Ol' Man River," from the musical *Show Boat*. Violence, however, erupted as soon as the audience began to leave the concert grounds. Waiting for the concertgoers at the exit were several thousand protesters, including members of local veterans groups. Yelling racial slurs and throwing rocks and bricks, the demonstrators smashed windshields and car windows, injuring nearly 150 people, several of them seriously. Although hundreds of state troopers and local police officers had been brought in to keep the peace, most simply stood by while concertgoers were attacked; a few police officers even took part in the violence. Robeson himself was hustled from the concert grounds in the backseat of a car whose windows had been covered with blankets.

Most American news accounts of the events of September 4 blamed the violence on the concert's leftist organizers, claiming they deliberately provoked the riots for propaganda purposes, rather than on the protesters. Unsurprisingly, given the strongly anti-Communist atmosphere in the United States at the time, none of the lawsuits filed against state officials on behalf of injured audience members, white or black, were successful. Within a year of the Peekskill riots, the State Department canceled Robeson's passport, declaring that it was not in the best interests of the country to let him travel abroad. Blacklisted at home and unable to earn a living in Europe where he remained popular, Robeson watched his annual income plummet to

On September 4, 1949, Paul Robeson sang his signature song, "Ol' Man River," at a concert in Peekskill, New York. The concert, organized as a benefit for the Civil Rights Congress, was scheduled to take place on August 27, but was rescheduled to September 4 due to protests. In the aftermath of the concert, riots broke out in which more than 100 people were injured.

almost nothing. After his passport was finally returned in 1958, Robeson spent the next five years giving concerts and traveling abroad, including several long visits to the Soviet Union, which he continued to hold up as a model of racial tolerance and economic and social equality. During the early 1960s, his physical and psychological health deteriorated sharply, and in 1963, Robeson decided to return to the United States for good. Until his death 13 years later, Robeson remained a virtual recluse in his sister's home in Philadelphia.

For many years after his death, Robeson was all but forgotten by the American public. By the last decade of the twentieth century, however, dozens of biographies, articles, and documentaries on the groundbreaking performer-activist had started to appear. Today, he is celebrated as a great performing artist, as well as a forerunner of the American civil rights and black pride movements and a tireless champion of laborers everywhere. Despite Robeson's unwillingness to acknowledge the dark side of the oppressive Soviet regime, which he continued to defend until his last days, he remains, more than a century after his birth, one of the most fascinating figures in American history and culture.

2

The Reverend Robeson's Son

Paul Leroy Robeson was born on April 9, 1898, in the college town of Princeton, New Jersey, the seventh and last child of 54-year-old William Drew Robeson, a Presbyterian minister, and 45-year-old Louisa Bustill Robeson. Two of the couple's children had died as infants nearly 20 years before Paul's birth. His surviving siblings included a sister, Marian, then age 4, and three brothers: Ben, age 6; Reeve, age 12; and Bill, age 17.

It was William Robeson "who more than anyone else influenced my life," Paul Robeson wrote in his book, *Here I Stand*, 40 years after his father's death: "I loved him like no one in all the world." By all accounts, the Reverend Robeson was a remarkable man. Born into slavery in 1844, William made a daring escape from the North Carolina plantation, where he toiled as a field hand, when he was just 15 years old. Guided by the courageous black and white volunteers of the Underground Railroad—a secret network that helped escaped slaves reach sanctuary in the free states of the North and Canada—William made his way to Pennsylvania. In 1861, the Civil War erupted, pitting the federal government against 11 Southern slave states determined to secede from the Union. William immediately volunteered for the Union army, although he, like other free blacks, would have been relegated to a labor battalion, digging ditches and carrying water for white soldiers, during the conflict's first year. Not until 1862 were African Americans permitted to take up arms for the Union cause.

Following the Union victory over the rebellious Southern slave states in 1865 and the outlawing of slavery throughout the nation the same year, William resolved to earn a college degree and enter the ministry. Having mastered the fundamentals of reading and writing at a Pennsylvania school for freed slaves, he enrolled in the college preparatory program at Lincoln University near Philadelphia in 1867. Founded in 1854, Lincoln was the first institution of higher education for blacks in the United States. In 1869, William received the equivalent of a high school degree from Lincoln's preparatory school, going on to earn his bachelor's degree from the university four years later. In 1876, at age 31, he graduated from Lincoln's School of Theology as an ordained Presbyterian minister.

Shortly after graduating, William married Louisa Bustill, a teacher at the Robert Vaux School in Philadelphia, the first public school for African Americans with an entirely black teaching staff. Twenty-three-year-old Louisa was considered quite a catch for William. Nearly six feet tall (182 centimeters) and strikingly attractive, she was widely admired for her keen intelligence and gracious dignity. She also belonged to one of the most prominent black families in Pennsylvania. Descendants of the Bantu people of sub-Saharan Africa, the Bustills married English Quakers and Lenape Indians after arriving in British America as slaves.

Louisa's great-grandfather, Cyrus Bustill, purchased his freedom from his Quaker master in 1769, when he was 37, and went

A painting of Harriet Tubman, one of the leaders of the Underground Railroad, as she escorts escaped slaves into Canada. The Underground Railroad was a network of secret routes and safe houses in the United States used by runaway slaves—including William Robeson, Paul Robeson's father—to escape to free Northern states and Canada in the years before the Civil War.

on to become a highly successful baker in Burlington, New Jersey, even supplying bread to George Washington's army during the Revolutionary War (1775–1783). Moving to Philadelphia after the war, Cyrus cofounded the first mutual aid (self-help) organization of American blacks, the Free African Society, in 1787. Over the next decades, the Bustill family produced an impressive array of educators, artists, scholars, and business owners and helped run the Underground Railroad in Pennsylvania. Paul Robeson later confided to friends that the Bustills had been disappointed by his mother's choice of husband because they looked down on William's poor and uneducated family. The Bustills' disapproval seems to have made little difference to the independent-minded Louisa, however. She threw herself wholeheartedly into her new life as the Reverend Robeson's wife, assisting William in his community work and in composing his weekly sermons.

THE REVEREND ROBESON'S RISE AND FALL IN PRINCETON

In 1878, William Robeson was called to serve as pastor of the Witherspoon Street Presbyterian Church in the central New Jersey town of Princeton, home to Princeton University. In many ways, the Princeton church was a plum assignment for the new clergyman. Racial prejudice was rampant in Princeton, as it was throughout much of the United States at the time. The vast majority of the college town's African-American residents, including most of William's parishioners, were relegated to low-paying jobs as day laborers or servants. Nonetheless, Princeton's black community was tightly knit and unusually large for central New Jersey. By the end of the nineteenth century, 900 of Princeton's approximately 5,000 inhabitants—nearly one-fifth of the population—were African American. Of the three black churches in Princeton, the Witherspoon Street Church had the largest congregation. Because of its close ties with the First Presbyterian Church, where many of the town's wealthiest white residents worshipped, it was also the most well-endowed black church in Princeton. In contrast to Princeton's other African-American churches, the Witherspoon Street Church boasted an auditorium and a spacious parsonage for its minister and his family.

When Paul Robeson was born in the Witherspoon Street parsonage in April 1898, William had been pastor of the church for nearly 20 years and was easily the most respected figure in Princeton's large black community. Paul once described his father "as a sort of bridge between the Have-nots and the Haves" of Princeton, serving "in many worldly ways—seeking work for the jobless, money for the needy, mercy from the Law." Yet, although he persuaded many of Princeton's leading citizens to provide financial and other forms of assistance to the town's downtrodden black residents over the years, William's outspoken support for racial equality sometimes got him into trouble with his white neighbors. William's black parishioners and neighbors would later remember the Reverend Robeson as a staunch civil rights activist. It was this unbending insistence on racial justice that may have been behind William's dismissal from his Princeton church in January 1901, when Paul was still a toddler.

The all-white presbytery—or body of ruling elders—for Presbyterian congregations in the greater Princeton area first began to try to push William out of his pulpit in January 1900. Right until the bitter end 12 months later, the presbytery's accusations against Robeson remained vague. One thing, however, is evident. While William enjoyed the nearly unanimous support of his congregation, by the turn of the century, he had managed to create a sense of "general unrest and dissatisfaction" among many of the well-to-do whites "who have been the Church's friends and helpers," according to the presbytery's official complaint against him. Some historians have suggested that a big public rally William held at his church in late 1899 to denounce a recent upsurge in lynchings of Southern blacks had alienated powerful members of Princeton's upper crust, many of whom had Southern roots.

TRAGEDY STRIKES THE ROBESONS

Whatever the real reason for the Reverend Robeson's removal from the Witherspoon Street Church in early 1901, the loss of his pulpit was a devastating blow for the Robeson family.

Soon after William's dismissal, the Robesons were forced to give up their comfortable home in the Witherspoon Street parsonage for a cramped and rundown house around the corner on Green Street. Unable to find a better job in Princeton, William bought a wagon and a mare and began to haul ashes for the town's prosperous white residents. Despite his dramatically changed circumstances, he accepted his situation with dignity and courage. His son later reminisced: "Not once did I hear him complain of the poverty and misfortune of those years. Not one word of bitterness ever came from him. Serene, undaunted, he struggled to earn a livelihood and to see to our education."

Three years after William lost his pulpit, the Robeson family suffered another, far more terrible calamity when Louisa died in a household accident. Over the past several years, cataracts had been progressively robbing Louisa of her eyesight. One day in January 1904, while she was cleaning beneath the family's coal-burning stove, a lump of coal fell onto her flowing skirts. Because she was nearly blind, she did not notice the smoldering coal until her clothing had already ignited. Eleven-year-old Ben, who had stayed home from school to help his mother clean, panicked when he saw her long skirt engulfed in flames and ran into the street, shouting for help. By the time a neighbor had arrived and doused the fire, Louisa had suffered third-degree burns to her feet, legs, and torso. She lingered for several hours in excruciating pain before dying from her injuries.

No one—including Paul himself—could later remember where he was on that awful January day, but his biographer Lloyd L. Brown thinks that the five-year-old was most likely at home and witnessed the entire traumatic episode. It was not only his mother's horrific accident and death, however, that Paul managed to block from his memory. In *Here I Stand*, Robeson confessed that he had no recollections of her whatsoever, "though my memory of other things goes back before her tragic death. . . . I remember . . . the funeral, and the relatives who came, but it must be that the pain and shock of her death blotted out all other personal recollections."

FROM PRINCETON TO WESTFIELD

In later years, Robeson fondly recalled the outpouring of love and support he received from his many relatives in Princeton and from the town's black community generally, following his mother's sudden death. He wrote in *Here I Stand*:

> There must have been moments when I felt the sorrows of a motherless child, but what I most remember from my youngest days was an abiding sense of comfort and security. I got plenty of mothering, not only from Pop and my brothers and sister when they were home, but from the whole of our close-knit community. Across the street and down each block were all my aunts and uncles and cousins—including some who were not actual relatives at all. . . . In a way I was "adopted" by all these good people, and there was always a place at their tables and a place in a bed . . . when my father was away.

In 1907, when Paul was nine, William was called to serve as pastor of a church in Westfield, 30 miles (48 kilometers) north of Princeton. The Westfield church, which belonged to the all-black African Methodist Episcopal Zion (AME Zion) denomination, was tiny and debt-ridden. Nonetheless, grateful for the opportunity to return to the ministry after six years without a pulpit, William lost no time in accepting the struggling congregation's invitation. Moving to Westfield must have been emotionally wrenching for Paul, since it meant leaving the loving Princeton relatives and neighbors who had nurtured and supported him since his mother's death. Westfield, however, did have one important advantage over Princeton. Although Westfield had fewer black residents, its working-class white majority was more accepting of African Americans than the wealthy college town's white elite. Robeson recalled that in his new hometown, "barriers between Negro and white existed, . . . but they were not so rigid; and . . . there were more friendly connections between the two groups." Black students were barred from all public schools in Princeton. In Westfield, however, Paul attended integrated elementary and junior high schools. There his outgoing personality, infectious smile, and exceptional athletic abilities made him popular among his classmates, white as well as black.

One of the most memorable events of Paul's youth occurred while he was living in Westfield: the first—and last—time he openly disobeyed his father. The incident took place when William was 63 and Paul was 10, and the only Robeson child still living at home. It was a story that Paul told over and over again as an adult, including in *Here I Stand*:

> My father told me to do something and I didn't do it. "Come here," he said; but I ran away. He ran after me. I darted across the road. He followed, stumbled and fell. I was horrified. I hurried back, helped Pop to his feet. He had knocked out one of his teeth. I have never forgotten the emotions—the sense of horror, shame, ingratitude, selfishness—that overwhelmed me. I adored him, would have given my life for him in a flash—and here I had hurt him, disobeyed him! Never did he have to admonish me again.

EXCELLING AT SOMERVILLE HIGH

Three years after moving to Westfield, William Robeson was offered another ministerial position at a larger AME Zion church in the rural community of Somerville, New Jersey, about 15 miles (24 kilometers) north of Princeton. In Somerville, Paul had to complete his junior high education at a segregated school. But in contrast to Princeton, Somerville's public high school was open to blacks. Paul and William lived in an overwhelmingly African-American and somewhat rundown section of Somerville seldom visited by most white townspeople. Nonetheless, as in Westfield, Paul's outstanding athletic skills and vibrant personality helped him attract a large circle of friends of both races, especially after he began to attend integrated Somerville High in 1911.

At Somerville High, Paul was one of just eight students out of a graduating class of 38 to take part in the college preparatory program, which included Latin, ancient history, and four years of English. In early twentieth-century America, only a small minority of whites, and even fewer blacks, continued their education beyond high school. William Robeson had high expectations for his children, however, and encouraged every one of them to follow in his footsteps and attend college.

Paul was determined to shine at Somerville High. He was a star of the football, baseball, basketball, track, and debate teams; served as sports editor for the school newspaper; and performed with the glee and drama clubs. Even with all of those activities, he still managed to earn top grades, graduating first in his class in 1915. His father demanded that he strive for nothing less than straight As. Robeson recalled years later:

> I have often told how he was never satisfied with a school mark of 95 when 100 was possible. But this was not because he made a fetish of perfection. Rather it was that the concept of *personal integrity*, which was his ruling passion, included inseparably the idea of *maximum human fulfillment*. Success in life was not to be measured in terms of money and personal advancement, but rather the goal must be the richest and highest development of one's own potential.

William Robeson kept a close eye on Paul's academic progress, taking an especially keen interest in helping him develop his public speaking skills. A talented orator himself, William started to train his son for public speaking when Paul was still a young child. After Paul joined Somerville High's debate team, William regularly gave him practice speeches to learn at home. "Line by line my father took me through them, dwelling on the choice of a word, the turn of a phrase, or the potency of an inflection," Robeson recalled: "Then, in the evenings I delivered my prepared orations to the family circle and received criticism and encouragement." Douglas Brown, a fellow debate team member, told an interviewer years later: "Paul had the artistic gift of projection and the flair to move people, the emotion and gift of speaking." During his senior year, Paul competed in a statewide oratorical contest. He won third

Paul Robeson's Siblings

Born during a time when blacks received little encouragement to continue their education past grade school, all of William Robeson's children not only graduated from high school but also attended college. Being able to attend high school at all was a challenge for the older Robeson children, since blacks were barred from Princeton's public high school. Bill and Reeve commuted to Trenton, 11 miles (18 kilometers) away, to attend high school, while Ben and Marian attended all-black private secondary schools in North Carolina, near William's parents.

Bill and Reeve attended William's alma mater, Lincoln University, though to William's disappointment, Reeve dropped out during his junior year. Reeve later moved to Detroit, where he reportedly died in poverty. Paul's other three siblings, however, went on to build successful professional careers. Ben studied for the ministry in North Carolina and became pastor of a church in Harlem in New York City. Marian finished her studies at a Pennsylvania college and became a schoolteacher in Philadelphia. Bill enrolled in the University of Pennsylvania Medical School after graduating from Lincoln, although he soon withdrew because he could not pay the high tuition bills. For many years, Bill Robeson supported himself as a Pullman porter, the only reliable work he could find, despite his college degree. In 1921, he finally earned his M.D. from the College of Medicine of Howard University, a historically black university in Washington, D.C., and worked as a physician in the nation's capital until his death four years later.

place for his recitation of a fiery speech by antislavery activist Wendell Phillips on Toussaint L'Ouverture (1743–1803), a former slave who led the Haitian Revolution against French rule.

"IN EVERY WAY THE EQUAL OF A WHITE MAN"

Paul was one of just a dozen blacks out of a student body of about 200, but for the most part, his years at Somerville High "passed unmarred by overt racial conflict," Sheila Tully Boyle and Andrew Bunie wrote in *Paul Robeson: The Years of Promise and Achievement.* His keen intelligence, remarkable aptitude for athletics, singing, and public speaking, and upbeat personality made him a favorite among the teaching staff as well as his fellow students. Years later, Robeson fondly recalled the Somerville teachers whose support had meant the most to him, including Miss Vosseller, his music instructor, who was deeply impressed by his powerful singing voice, and Miss Miller, his English teacher, who encouraged his budding interest in acting.

During his high school years, however, Paul was not left completely unscathed by racial bigotry. Friend and teammate Douglas Brown later remembered that the other Somerville football players made a point of watching out for Paul, whom Brown described as 90 percent of the team, when they had to play in the neighboring town of Phillipsburg. Racist community members had reportedly promised a box of cigars to the Phillipsburg player who could knock Somerville's six-foot-two-inch-tall (188-centimeter-tall) star fullback out cold. According to Brown, at the Phillipsburg game, Paul "refused to show his feelings when the crowd yelled racial slurs at him, just played hard. He was in every respect much bigger than those who were racially snide with him, and he was not going to let himself be thrown off pace by their remarks."

During his senior year, Paul encountered racism closer to home when Somerville hired a new principal, Dr. Evans Ackerman. Paul was convinced that Ackerman despised him, despite—or, more likely, because of—his stellar academic and athletic record, and relished any opportunity to put him in his place. "He never spoke to me except to administer a reprimand and he seemed constantly to be looking for an excuse to do so," Robeson recalled. Because he had always believed that everything would go smoothly for him at Somerville as long as he "acted right," treating school authorities with unfailing "courtesy and restraint," Ackerman's attitude came as a shock to him. Robeson recalled:

> The better I did, the worse his scorn. The cheers of my fellow students as I played fullback on the football team—"Let Paul carry the ball! Yay-Paul!"—seemed to curdle the very soul of Dr. Ackerman; and when the music teacher made me soloist of the glee club, it was against the principal's furious opposition.

Ackerman's unrelenting hostility only served to make Paul more determined to show the principal, and anyone else who shared his racist views, that "the Negro was in every way the equal of the white man," as his father had always taught him. Thus, when Paul heard about a statewide competitive examination for a four-year scholarship to Rutgers College, a prestigious and overwhelmingly white college in New Brunswick, New Jersey, he resolved to take the test, even though he had been planning to attend his father's alma mater, Lincoln University. Students took the lengthy exam in two parts—the first part at the end of their junior year and the second late in their senior year. Since Paul was unaware of the scholarship when he was a junior, he had to take the exam all at once, in the same amount of time that his competitors had to complete only the senior portion. "The extra hurdle called for extraordinary effort," Paul wrote, "and I studied hard until late at night." Ackerman's "illwill," every bit as much as the "good wishes" of his teachers, classmates, and family, spurred him on, he later recalled.

Paul performed so well on the examination that he won the scholarship. It was "a decisive point in my life," he revealed in *Here I Stand.*

> That I would go to Rutgers was the least of it, for I was sure I'd be happier at Lincoln. The important thing was this: *Deep in my heart from that day on was a conviction which none of the Ackermans of America would ever be able to shake.* Equality might be denied, but I *knew* I was not inferior.

3

At Rutgers

When Paul Robeson entered Rutgers College in New Brunswick, New Jersey, in 1915, he was only the third African American to attend the all-male school since its founding 150 years earlier. During the early twentieth century, only a small percentage of those African Americans who went to college attended predominantly white schools. The vast majority enrolled at historically black institutions like Lincoln University, where Robeson had originally planned to go.

Shortly after arriving at Rutgers in September 1915, Robeson met with the head football coach, George Foster Sanford, to discuss the team's tryouts. Sanford was well aware of Robeson's stellar football career in nearby Somerville and believed he would be an asset to Rutgers's program. Despite Robeson's reputation as an outstanding athlete, however, some veteran players were dead set against having a black player on the team, Sanford warned. Undaunted, Robeson was determined to try out anyway. In an extensive interview with the *New York Times* in 1944, he could still vividly recall the brutal treatment he endured on the practice field the day after his meeting with Sanford:

> Rutgers had a great team that year, but the boys—well— they didn't want a Negro on their team, they just didn't want me on it. . . . On the first day of scrimmage they set about making sure that I wouldn't get on their team. One boy slugged me in the face and smashed my nose. . . . And then when I was down, flat on my back, another boy got me with his knee, just came over and fell on me. He managed to dislocate my right shoulder. . . .
>
> Broken nose, shoulder thrown out, and plenty of other cuts and bruises. . . . Seventeen years old, it was tough going for that age. . . . But my father . . . had impressed upon me that when I was out on a football field or in a classroom or anywhere else I wasn't there just on my own. I was the representative of a lot of Negro boys who wanted to play football and wanted to go to college, and as their representative, I had to show that I could take whatever was handed out.
>
> Well, I didn't know. My brother Bill came to see me, and he said, "Kid, I know what it is, I went through it at [the University of] Pennsylvania. If you want to quit school go ahead, but I wouldn't like to think, and our father wouldn't like to think, that our family had a quitter in it."
>
> So I stayed. I had ten days in bed, a few days at the training table, and then out for another scrimmage. I made a tackle and was on the ground. A boy came over and stepped hard on my hand. He meant to break the bones. The bones held, but his cleats took every single one of the fingernails off my right hand. . . . That's when I knew rage!
>
> The next play came around my end, the whole first string backfield came at me. I swept out my arms, and the three men running interference went down. The ball car-

rier was a first-class back named Kelly. I got Kelly in my two hands and I got him up over my head. I was going to smash him so hard to the ground that I'd break him right in two, and I could have done it. But just then Coach Sanford yelled: "Robey, you're on the varsity!" That brought me around.

BECOMING "ROBESON OF RUTGERS"

Robeson spent his first football season at Rutgers as a substitute tackle. Playing in four out of eight games, Robeson—or "Robey" as his teammates called him—so distinguished himself that he was singled out for special praise by Coach Sanford at the end-of-the-season banquet. Robeson's fellow players quickly came to admire the 17-year-old freshman's remarkable power, agility, and tenacity on the field, too. According to his son, Paul Robeson Jr., in *The Undiscovered Paul Robeson: An Artist's Journey 1898–1939*, as his white teammates' respect for him grew, they "even protected him from attempted fouls by opponents who were especially hostile to the first black player they had ever faced."

During his sophomore season, Robeson played guard and first-string tackle in all but one of Rutgers's seven football games. The one game he missed was Rutgers's matchup against Virginia's Washington and Lee University on October 14. The Southern team insisted that it would not play if Rutgers included a black man in its starting lineup. Eager to avoid trouble, college officials pressured Sanford to bench Robeson. Deeply upset by his exclusion from the game, Robeson considered transferring out of Rutgers. When he told his father, however, William vetoed the idea at once. Although the Reverend Robeson was his son's biggest fan, cheering him on at all of his home games, he sternly informed Paul that he had not gone to college just to play football.

Robeson, who participated in all of Rutgers's nine games during his junior season, emerged as a national college foot-

Paul Robeson was an All-American football player at Rutgers University in New Brunswick, New Jersey, in 1918. Although many of his white teammates did not want to play alongside a black player, Robeson won their respect through his tenacity and hard work.

ball star that year. Playing both offense and defense, "Robey" helped his team finish the 1917 season with seven wins, one tie, and one loss. His versatility and athleticism were so exceptional that the press started to refer to him as "The Magnificent Robeson." Although he was officially identified in Rutgers's starting lineup as an end, that classification was in name only, as an admiring sports commentator observed in the *Philadelphia Public Ledger* in 1918:

> [Robeson] is everything and everywhere. He is never in the same position in two plays. He is usually on the end, around which the runner sweeps, or if it is an off-tackle thrust or plunge between tackle and guard, he takes a position inside the end. . . . When Rutgers receives a kickoff the tall Negro is placed on the 10-yard line just in front of the goal posts, in the best position to take the ball. He catches the ball naturally and gracefully, handling it like a feather. He runs with an amble, his long strides covering ground very fast. . . . His great strength and weight [210 pounds, or 95 kilograms] make him a hard man to stop.

Walter Camp, the leading authority of his day on football, placed Robeson at the top of his list of College Stars of 1917. Each year for the previous two decades, Camp had selected an All-America team, made up of those football players he judged best for each position on a squad. He had planned to name Robeson as an All-American in 1917. Because the United States was fighting in World War I that year, Camp thought it more fitting to choose an All-Service team composed only of military members instead of picking a collegiate All-America team. Shortly after World War I ended in November 1918, Camp named Robeson as an All-American end for his 1918 dream team, a position no one in the history of football had ever played as well as Robeson, in Camp's opinion.

RACIAL SLIGHTS AND PERSONAL TRIUMPHS

Besides playing football, Robeson was the first black athlete on three other sports teams at Rutgers. He was a top scorer on the basketball team and took part in two spring sports: baseball and track and field. More than once, a Rutgers baseball game was held up because Robeson, the team's catcher, was scheduled to throw the javelin or discus in a track and field competition. By the end of his senior year, Robeson had managed to earn 12 varsity letters in his various sports, a college record.

Aside from his participation in sports, Robeson was involved in fewer extracurricular activities at Rutgers than at Somerville High School. Football was extremely popular at Rutgers, and Robeson's status as the team's star player, combined with his friendly and vibrant personality, won him the respect and affection of the college's overwhelmingly white student body. Nonetheless, his skin color restricted his extracurricular opportunities and social life at Rutgers. For instance, not a single Rutgers fraternity rushed Robeson, who was also strongly discouraged from joining the glee club, though his rich, deep voice was widely admired when he sang at local churches.

His exclusion from Rutgers's all-white glee club was "undoubtedly because of the socializing . . . that followed performances," authors Sheila Tully Boyle and Andrew Bunie wrote. In the early twentieth century, African Americans were barred from most public restaurants and hotels in the United States, not only in the South but in the more racially tolerant North as well. Robeson was far and away the football team's best known and valuable player. Nonetheless, he was barred from attending New Brunswick's yearly civic banquet for the Rutgers football team because the dinner was traditionally held at a local hotel where African Americans were unwelcome. "Whenever there was a banquet for the team, Paul always arranged, gracefully, to have some other place to go," his former teammate, Bill Feitner, told author Lloyd Brown years later. "For the most part Robeson said nothing about these slights,"

Boyle and Bunie wrote. "Every now and then, he talked with his friend Fritz Pollard [a black football player at a predominantly white college in Rhode Island]. . . . But, generally, Paul absorbed the full impact of these experiences himself."

One extracurricular activity aside from sports in which he did find warm acceptance during his college career was public speaking. Robeson was the undisputed star of the Rutgers varsity debate team, handily winning the annual class oratorical contest from his freshman through his senior year. For him, the most meaningful of the many oratorical awards he collected as a student was the first prize he won for extemporaneous, or impromptu, speaking during the spring of his junior year.

Robeson received the speaking award just three days after the death of his father on May 17, 1918, following a brief illness. Father and son had remained extremely close since he enrolled at Rutgers, even though the younger Robeson lived

IN HIS OWN WORDS...

Throughout his life, Paul Robeson was closer to the Robeson clan than to his mother's family, the Bustills. Shortly after his father's death in 1918, however, he decided to attend a Bustill family reunion in Philadelphia. Leafing through his college scrapbook years later, Robeson discovered a reunion program that listed him as one of the speakers. While he had long forgotten what he said that day, he realized from the speech's title that the talk must have focused on what he viewed as the central theme of his father's life—an unswerving commitment to his ideals:

> I cannot recall anything I said in my speech on that occasion, though I did jot down in my scrapbook its title—"Loyalty to Convictions." That I chose this topic was not accidental, for that was the text of my father's life—loyalty to one's convictions. Unbending. Despite anything. From my youngest days I was imbued with this concept. This bedrock idea of integrity was taught by Reverend Robeson to his children not so much by preachment . . . but rather, by the daily example of his life and work.

on campus during the academic year and spent his summer breaks in Rhode Island, waiting tables at a seaside resort to help pay for his college expenses. Most Sundays while he was at Rutgers, he returned to nearby Somerville to attend William's church, where he often sang solos during services. He knew that his father—who had devoted countless hours to coaching him in public speaking during his high school years—had been greatly looking forward to his latest oratorical competition. Consequently, he vowed to go through with the speech competition as a tribute to his adored parent. An article in the May 23, 1918, edition of the Somerville *Unionist Gazette* noted Robeson's triumph in the contest:

> Paul Leroy Robeson, son of the late Rev. W.D. Robeson, . . . added another to his string of honors by winning the Junior Exhibition at Rutgers on Monday evening. Because of his father's death it was feared that Paul would be unable to enter the contest, but as it was his father's wish he decided to do so. . . . Paul's subject was, "Loyalty and the American Negro," and he waxed eloquent on the part the American Negro had played in past wars.

"A NAME AND A RECORD EQUALED BY NONE"

At the end of his junior year at Rutgers, Robeson received another even more prestigious honor than the annual oratorical prize when he was made a member of the nation's oldest academic honor society, Phi Beta Kappa. The distinction he later recalled treasuring most from his Rutgers years, however, was not his Phi Beta Kappa key, but his induction into the college's senior honor society, Cap and Skull, in the spring of 1919. Each year, members of the graduating class chose four seniors who they believed best embodied the ideals of Rutgers for the Cap and Skull Award. According to Robeson's classmate, Malcolm Pitt, the award "was the most important of all honors as it was given only to those seniors exemplifying

"The New Idealism"

Entitled "The New Idealism," Paul Robeson's valedictory address to the Rutgers Class of 1919 discussed the many challenges confronting Americans in the post–World War I era, but it focused primarily on the issue of race relations. In his speech, Robeson expressed the hope that black Americans, who had recently fought side-by-side with white Americans, would be rewarded for their World War I service by receiving equal rights and opportunities at home:

Today we feel that America has proved true to her trust. Realizing that there were worse things than war; that the liberties won through long years of travail were too sacred to be thrown away, . . . we paid again, in part, the price of liberty. In the fulfillment of our country's duty to civilization, in its consecrating of all resources to the attainment of the ideal America, in the triumph of right over the forces of autocracy, we see the development of a new spirit, a new motive power in American life. . . .

We of the younger generation especially must feel a sacred call to that which lies before us. . . . We of this less favored [black] race realize that our future lies chiefly in our own hands. On ourselves alone will depend the preservation of our liberties and the transmission of them in their integrity to those who will come after us. . . . We know that neither institutions nor friends can make a race stand unless it has strength in its own foundation; that races like individuals must stand or fall by their own merit; that to fully succeed they must practice their virtues of self-reliance, self-respect, industry, perseverance, and economy.

But in order for us to successfully do all these things it is necessary that you of the favored [white] race catch a new vision and exemplify in your actions this new American spirit. That spirit which prompts you to compassion, . . . embodying the desire to relieve the manifest distress of your fellows; that motive which realizes as the task of civilization the achievement of happiness and the institution of community spirit. . . .

And may I not appeal to you . . . to join with us in continuing to fight for the great principles for which they contended, until in all sections of this fair land there will be equal opportunities for all, and character shall be the standard of excellence; until men by constructive work aim toward Solon's definition of the ideal government—where an injury to the meanest citizen is an insult to the whole constitution; and until black and white shall clasp friendly hands in the consciousness of the fact that we are brethren and that God is the father of us all.

excellence in all facets of Rutgers life."

Shortly before the start of his senior year, Robeson decided to attend law school after receiving his undergraduate degree. Coach Sanford, his closest friend and counselor on the Rutgers faculty since his freshman year, probably had a great deal to do with Robeson's choice of career path. According to Lloyd Brown, when Robeson, still grieving his father's death, returned to Rutgers in the autumn of 1918,

> an even closer relationship developed between him and the football coach, who now became something of a foster-father to the young man.... It is likely that Sanford played an important part in Paul's decision to prepare for law school. Sanford himself was a lawyer, though not a practicing one, and he later influenced his son . . . to earn a law degree.

Brown thinks that the example of Rutgers's first African-American graduate, James Carr, who became an attorney after graduating from Columbia Law School, may also have inspired Robeson to study law.

When Robeson graduated with the nearly 100 other members of the Rutgers Class of 1919 on June 10, he had received a remarkable array of honors. Besides his election to the Phi Beta Kappa and Cap and Skull societies, and his many athletic awards, he had been inducted into the college Literary Society, received Rutgers's annual oratorical prize four times, and been selected as class valedictorian. Asked to address the senior class at the commencement ceremony, Robeson delivered a widely praised speech that touched on the challenges and opportunities facing black Americans of the era. According to Paul Robeson Jr., many members of his father's audience "would later assert that no commencement orator in the history of Rutgers College had received such long applause."

The lead editorial in the June 1919 issue of *The Targum*, Rutgers's student newspaper, focused on the school's most famous graduate to date, Paul Robeson. Robeson, the editors proclaimed, had "made a name and a record equaled by none" during his four years as the college's star athlete-scholar. In concluding their glowing assessment of his many accomplishments at Rutgers, the *Targum* editors called on Robeson to be a leader and role model to all African Americans:

> Now, Paul, as you pass from our midst, take with you the respect and appreciation of us who remain behind. May your success in life be comparable to that of college days. In you the other members of your race may well find a noble example, and this leadership is your new duty.
>
> May Rutgers never forget this noble son and may he always remember his Alma Mater.

4

From Law Student to Actor

Two months after graduating from Rutgers in 1919, Paul Robeson left New Jersey for New York City, where he found an apartment in Harlem and prepared to start law school at New York University (NYU) in the fall. Once an all-white enclave, Harlem then was well on its way to becoming the foremost black residential and cultural center in the northern United States.

African Americans had begun to flock to Harlem in large numbers a decade before Robeson arrived in the Upper Manhattan neighborhood. Many came from the South—home to 90 percent of the African-American population in 1900—as part of the so-called Great Migration of more than a million Southern blacks who headed to northern cities from 1910 to 1930. Confronted with widespread lynching, exclusion from voting, and severely restricted employment and educational opportunities in the South, they hoped to build a better life for themselves and their children in the North's industrial centers. Martin Duberman observed in *Paul Robeson: A Biography*:

> No promised land awaited the new migrants to the North, yet amid the endemic squalor and discrimination they did manage to make some improvements in their daily lot: decreased death, illiteracy, and infant-mortality rates, a rise in school enrollment and political participation (blacks could vote in the North). Fierce white resistance to residential integration—including bombings and beatings—forced blacks into ghettos, where the development of community institutions like churches and fraternal orders provided some sense of refuge, a potential political base, and a focus for cultural cohesion.

Across the United States, race violence rose to never-before-seen heights throughout the summer of 1919, when Robeson moved to Harlem. During what would come to be called the "Red Summer," brutal attacks on African Americans skyrocketed in many U.S. cities. Yet Harlem, like the rest of New York City, remained peaceful in 1919. In July, many leading black activists organized a huge march in Manhattan to protest the growing bloodshed in Chicago, Philadelphia, and other cities. Some 10,000 black men and women, most of them residents of Harlem, marched in silent solidarity down Fifth Avenue in an attempt to pressure the U.S. Congress into passing legislation to protect African Americans from racially motivated attacks. Although Southern congressmen successfully blocked passage of the proposed legislation, the epidemic of mass violence against African Americans in U.S. cities died down during the following months, in large part because of increasing black resistance to white mobs.

Harlem's rapidly expanding African-American community was angered but not disheartened by the antiblack violence

In 1919, the year Paul Robeson moved to the New York City neighborhood of Harlem, 10,000 African Americans marched in silent protest against a spate of lynchings that occurred across the United States that summer.

of the Red Summer and the government's refusal to take a strong stand against the attacks. For the neighborhood's new black majority, "the goals of self-improvement and economic advancement appeared within reach," authors Sheila Tully Boyle and Andrew Bunie explained. "In Harlem, as in no other part of the country, there was hope." By 1919, many of the country's most respected and successful black citizens had moved to Harlem, including the Reverend Adam Clayton Powell Sr., the prominent author and clergyman; and Madam C.J. Walker, the wealthy businesswoman. Harlem was also home to the largest branches of the country's two leading civil rights organizations, the National Association for the Advancement of Colored People (NAACP) and the National Urban League, and several major black periodicals, including the NAACP's magazine, *The Crisis.*

When Paul Robeson arrived in Harlem, the neighborhood was a nationally recognized political and business center for America's black population. It was also rapidly becoming home to the "Harlem Renaissance," an African-American cultural movement associated with such internationally renowned figures as poet Langston Hughes; writer and social activist W.E.B. Du Bois; and blues singer Bessie Smith. From the very start, Robeson was connected to Harlem's flourishing cultural scene; his first roommates in the neighborhood were two struggling young actors and musicians, Clarence Muse and James Lightfoot. Robeson also quickly became acquainted with a number of Harlem's more established cultural figures, along with local business and civil rights leaders, who were eager to meet the celebrated college football star and Phi Beta Kappa honoree. For many of Harlem's cultural and social elite, the young scholar-athlete seemed the very model of the "New Negro"—an early twentieth-century term for educated and ambitious African Americans who sought to prove through their own accomplishments that blacks were equal to whites.

LAW SCHOOL AND PRO FOOTBALL

Although NYU had awarded Robeson a sizable scholarship, he quickly became dissatisfied with his choice of law school. By the end of his first term, he was convinced that he would be happier in Columbia University's law program because of what he considered as Columbia's more intellectual atmosphere and because its campus was closer to Harlem. In January 1920, therefore, having received special permission from the dean of the Columbia School of Law to enter its program mid-year, Robeson transferred.

Since Columbia awarded Robeson no scholarship money, he was forced to juggle several part-time jobs to cover his tuition and living expenses. Rental fees in Harlem were high at the time, because many landlords in most other Manhattan neighborhoods refused to take African-American tenants. During Robeson's first semester at Columbia, he earned money by working the night shift at the post office; singing at private parties, church fundraisers, and local community events; and tutoring college students in Latin.

By the autumn of 1920, Robeson had decided to supplement his spotty income by playing part time in the new American Professional Football League, soon to be renamed the National Football League (NFL). He played for two professional teams: the Akron Pros, during the 1921 season, and the Milwaukee Badgers, during the 1922 season, commuting to his games by overnight train.

In the early 1920s, professional football was much less popular than college football, and professional players were not well paid. In fact, in the earliest days of the pro leagues, team practices were optional and most players worked at other jobs during the week. Nonetheless, the money that Robeson was able to make per game went a long way toward paying his tuition and rent. In later years, Robeson seldom talked about his pro football career. Perhaps that was because during his time with Akron, he and his fellow black teammate and friend, Fritz Pollard, had to put up with a lot in return for their paychecks. Martin Duberman wrote:

> Akron, a factory town employing many white Southern migrants, was known for its overt, unapologetic racism. Fritz Pollard later remembered the raucous boos of the fans, the inability to get a hotel room or a meal in a restaurant, and the need to dress for games in [Pros' owner] Frank Nied's cigar factory.

ESLANDA CARDOZO GOODE

Toward the end of his sophomore year at Rutgers, Robeson had fallen in love with a vivacious young black woman named Gerry Neale, from the nearby town of Freehold. They saw a great deal of each other over the next several years, even after she enrolled as a student at Howard University in Washington, D.C. Decades later Neale revealed to Paul Robeson Jr. that she had loved his father deeply, but she repeatedly turned down Robeson's proposals of marriage. "Even that far back I understood that he was a man of destiny and that he would belong to the world, rather than to his family," she told Paul Jr. in 1976. "He was wonderful to be with, and yet I couldn't live with a man like that."

Gerry Neale may have been reluctant to wed him, but plenty of other women clearly viewed the famed "Robeson of Rutgers" as an outstanding marital prospect. Contemporaries remembered the handsome young law student as being very popular with the opposite sex, recalling that he could often be seen strolling down the streets of Harlem with an admiring young woman on his arm. Indeed, that is exactly what Robeson was doing when his future wife, Eslanda "Essie" Cardozo Goode, first set eyes on him shortly after he moved to Harlem, where Goode also lived. "Paul was making his way down Seventh Avenue one glorious summer afternoon in 1919 with a pretty girl on his arm; he was greeting friends and admirers along the way with his wide engaging smile," Goode later reminisced in her diary. She wrangled an introduction to Robeson from his date, a childhood acquaintance of hers, and soon after, Essie and Paul began to date regularly.

A year and a half older than Paul, Goode was a successful career woman when she met Robeson. Ambitious and self-assured, she was the proud granddaughter of one of the post–Civil War era's most prominent African Americans, Francis Lewis Cardozo, the illegitimate son of a wealthy South

Carolinian of Spanish-Jewish descent and his mixed black–
Native American mistress. After attending college in Scotland
and being ordained a minister in the Presbyterian Church,
Cardozo worked as a pastor and a teacher in Connecticut.
During Reconstruction—the period when Union troops were
stationed in the defeated Southern states from 1865 to 1877—
he returned to South Carolina, where he ran a school for
newly freed slaves. In 1868, Cardozo became the first African
American to hold a statewide political office when he was
elected secretary of state of South Carolina. After holding that
post for four years, he served as secretary of the treasury of
South Carolina. Cardozo's political career came to an abrupt
end in 1877, when Union troops pulled out of the South and
South Carolina's new segregationist governor promptly dis-
missed the black treasury secretary. Moving to Washington,
D.C., Cardozo became the principal of one of the country's
top secondary schools for African Americans.

In 1890, Francis's daughter and Essie's mother, Eslanda
Cardozo, married John Goode, a clerk in the War Department.
In 1902, when Essie, their third and last child, was six, John
died, leaving Eslanda Goode to support their young brood on
her own. The scholar of her family, Essie graduated from high
school in just three years and won a full tuition scholarship to
attend the University of Illinois, where she majored in chem-
istry. After transferring to Columbia University for her senior
year, she accepted a job as a laboratory technician at New
York's prestigious Presbyterian Hospital. Soon she had worked
her way up to the post of chief histological chemist in the
Surgical Pathological Laboratory. Never before had an African
American—or a woman of any race—held such an important
post at Presbyterian Hospital.

Although Robeson was attracted to Essie's quick mind
and exotic good looks, it was soon clear that she was more
infatuated with him than he was with her. Even a year after
they began to date, Robeson was still clinging to the hope

that Gerry Neale would change her mind about marrying him. Essie, though, was not one to be discouraged easily. After their first meeting in Harlem, she launched a carefully calculated "campaign to win Paul," as she later confessed in her book, *American Argument*. In the summer of 1921, shortly after Robeson failed one last time to persuade Gerry to be his wife, Essie finally achieved her goal when he proposed to her instead. Deciding to forgo a formal wedding, the couple was quietly married by a justice of the peace on August 17, 1921.

A BRIEF LEGAL CAREER

After graduating from Columbia Law School in early 1923, Robeson was hired by an all-white New York law firm headed by fellow Rutgers alumni Louis Stotesbury. Although Stotesbury appreciated Robeson's keen intelligence and meticulous attention to detail, "just about everyone else at the firm went out of their way to register their hostility in a variety of small ways," Paul Robeson Jr. contended. Robeson chose to overlook the nearly constant slights until a racist secretary angrily refused to take dictation from him.

According to Robeson Jr., when his father explained what had happened to Stotesbury, his boss

> listened sympathetically, indicating that he could readily eliminate the worst aspects of Paul's mistreatment by the staff; however, he was frank in addressing the broader and far more intractable racial discrimination that Paul would face in the legal profession: Present and future white clients would not agree to have a "colored man" as their trial lawyer, and many judges would be prejudiced against him because of his race.

Unwilling to accept the limited opportunities available to him as a black lawyer in early twentieth-century America, Robeson decided by the end of 1923 to give up the legal profession to pursue a very different career path. With the strong support of his new wife, he resolved to try his luck as a professional actor.

EARLY ACTING EXPERIENCES

Essie had been encouraging Robeson to develop what she considered to be his natural talent for acting since their dating days, when he had accepted the lead role in an amateur theater production at the Harlem branch of the YWCA, entitled *Simon the Cyrenian*. During the summer of 1920, his friend Dora Cole Norman, a Harlem producer, had asked him to star in the drama about Simon of Cyrene, the man who helped Jesus carry the cross to Mount Calvary (also known as Golgotha) where the Romans crucified him. Although Robeson had only agreed to appear in the play as a favor to Norman and did not take his performance seriously, many of those who attended the production, including Essie, were greatly impressed by his rich, expressive speaking voice and natural stage presence.

Despite the positive response to his performance in *Simon*, Robeson did not return to the stage for another two years. Between his law studies and part-time football career, his schedule was already hectic enough. In the spring of 1922, however, Robeson decided to give the theater another try when he was offered his first professional acting role in a new drama called *Taboo*, about a black minstrel who was also an African voodoo king. With the pro-football season over for the year, the idea of making some extra money appealed to Robeson, even though he found the play's script confusing and amateurish. As it turned out, the critics agreed with Robeson's assessment of the play, which lasted just four performances before folding. Undeterred, *Taboo*'s wealthy white author, Mary Hoyt Wiborg, arranged a revival of the drama, renamed *Voodoo*, in England for the summer of 1922. With his wife's encouragement, Robeson decided to accept Wiborg's invitation to tour the English countryside with *Voodoo*.

English critics panned Wiborg's play, although most had positive words for Robeson's performance, particularly for his melodious, bass-baritone voice. Although he had little regard for the play, Robeson was glad that he went on the *Voodoo* tour. In England he encountered far less overt racial prejudice than back home in the United States. According to Lloyd Brown, the nearly universal kindliness and courtesy with which *Voodoo*'s black cast members were treated during the play's English run made him "feel more at home in their country than he would ever feel as a touring performer in his own homeland."

AN IMPORTANT AND CONTROVERSIAL NEW ROLE

Within a year of returning home from England in September 1922, Robeson had decided to give up on the law to focus on his budding acting career. Essie enthusiastically backed his decision. Not only was she convinced that he had genuine acting talent, but like her husband, she had also come to believe that his chances for success as an African-American lawyer were bleak.

In late 1923, Robeson got his first big break as an actor when Eugene O'Neill, one of America's most acclaimed playwrights, offered him the starring role in his new drama about interracial marriage, *All God's Chillun Got Wings*. O'Neill had heard glowing reports about Robeson from several members of the Provincetown Players, a New York–based theater group with which the playwright was associated. *All God's Chillun* was scheduled to open in the winter of 1924 at the Provincetown Players' theater in Greenwich Village. The production, however, and particularly the casting of Robeson as the male lead, attracted so much negative publicity that the opening of *All God's Chillun* was delayed until the following May.

In 1924, the idea of a romantic relationship between a black person and a white person was highly controversial. In fact, interracial marriage was illegal in 30 of America's then-48 states. Even four decades later, 17 Southern states still banned mixed-race unions. It was not until 1967 that the U.S. Supreme Court ruled that statutes prohibiting interracial marriages were unconstitutional. Because *All God's Chillun* included a scene in which the black protagonist, Jim Harris, kisses the hand of his white wife, Ella, casting an African American in the production, rather than a white actor in black makeup, aroused even more racist passions than the play's unconventional plot line. (Traditionally, all black speaking parts in mainstream theater productions were given to whites. Although O'Neill had broken with that tradition in 1920 by casting an African-American actor, Charles Gilpin, as the lead in his drama *The Emperor Jones*, that play did not deal with interracial love.)

The first newspaper reports in January 1924 of Robeson's casting as Jim Harris caused an immediate uproar, particularly in the South. O'Neill, Robeson, and the play's white female lead, Mary Blair, received menacing letters, including from Ku Klux Klan groups, threatening to kill family members or bomb the Provincetown Playhouse unless the production was canceled. As the play's scheduled opening approached, sensationalist newspaper articles warned of violent racial riots in New York City. When the play's understandably overwrought female star developed pleurisy, a lung infection sometimes linked to emotional stress, however, the much-anticipated opening of *All God's Chillun* had to be delayed indefinitely.

BRUTUS JONES AND JIM HARRIS

By April, with Mary Blair still unable to perform, the Provincetown Players decided to divert the public's attention from the controversy over *All God's Chillun* by reviving O'Neill's *The Emperor Jones*, with Robeson in the starring role of Brutus Jones. Robeson had just two weeks to learn all his lines for the play's opening on May 6. Yet he jumped at the chance to portray Jones, a character with considerably more complexity than Jim Harris. Although Brutus Jones, the self-proclaimed

In this September 1925 photo, Paul Robeson is seen performing in a production of Eugene O'Neill's play *Emperor Jones* at the Ambassadors' Theatre. His riveting take on the title character helped cement his reputation as a serious actor.

black ruler of a Caribbean island, has many flaws, the character is powerful, resourceful, and supremely confident, in sharp contrast to the weak-willed and insecure Harris.

Robeson's electrifying portrayal of Jones in the Provincetown Players' production of O'Neill's play was a huge hit with audiences and theater critics. A reviewer for the *New York Telegram and Evening Mail* cheered: "Robeson held his audience enthralled. . . . He has a powerful voice that fairly booms, and it is resonant. . . . [Robeson] is as fine an actor as there is

Body and Soul

In late 1924, Oscar Micheaux, the leading African-American film producer and director of the silent movie era, hired Paul Robeson to star in his newest project, *Body and Soul*. According to historian Cary D. Wintz in *Harlem Speaks: A Living History of the Harlem Renaissance*, "scholars today refer to this and similar films as 'race films' because they were produced by black filmmakers for black audiences. At the time almost no whites saw these films, which were shown in theaters that catered almost entirely to black audiences."

Robeson's first film was neither a box office nor a critical success within the African-American community. In *Body and Soul*, which featured an almost entirely black cast, Robeson played a dual role: that of identical twins with nothing in common except their physical appearance. One twin was a hardworking and kindly inventor. The other was a greedy, lecherous, and hard-drinking preacher, who used his natural charisma to take advantage of his naïve parishioners. The movie's extremely negative portrayal of the African-American clergy deeply offended many blacks. Consequently, black reviewers universally blasted the film and most black moviegoers shunned it, despite Robeson's celebrity status as a former college football star and an up-and-coming stage actor. Both Paul and Essie, who had persuaded her husband to appear in *Body and Soul* in the first place, were deeply embarrassed by his association with the film and avoided discussing the project publicly for the rest of their lives. Although the Robesons could not have foreseen it, some African-American film critics have developed a new respect for Robeson's first movie in recent years, hailing *Body and Soul* as "a breakthrough in that it 'wrestled with the complex nature of the black community,'" according to authors Sheila Tully Boyle and Andrew Bunie.

on the American stage." His rave notices for *The Emperor Jones* marked a critical turning point in his fledgling stage career. Not only did the glowing reviews give Robeson a new sense of confidence in his abilities as an actor, they practically ensured that he would be offered other major roles in the future.

On May 15, *All God's Chillun Got Wings* finally opened at the Provincetown Playhouse. To the surprise of Robeson, Blair, and everyone else involved in the production, there was no violence: Not even a single protester picketed the heavily

Directed by Oscar Micheaux, the silent 1925 film *Body and Soul*, in which Paul Robeson portrayed the Reverend Isaiah T. Jenkins *(seen here)* and his twin brother, was Robeson's first foray into filmmaking. Although Robeson was unhappy with the film, *Body and Soul* has gained new respect among African-American film critics in recent years.

policed theater on opening night or throughout the play's three-week run. Although *All God's Chillun* was financially successful, most critics, while praising Robeson's performance as Jim, found the plot and characterization feeble and below O'Neill's usual standards. Nor was the play well received by much of the black community. The racist response to both Robeson's casting and the play's interracial love scenes during the months leading up to its opening rallied a number of top black civil rights activists behind the production, including James Weldon Johnson, the secretary of the NAACP. But many African Americans were highly critical of the play itself and Robeson's decision to appear in it, complaining that the deeply insecure Jim Harris was a poor representative of their race. Some were even unhappy with Robeson's willingness to portray Brutus Jones because of the character's numerous moral shortcomings, including his seemingly unquenchable greed for money. Although Robeson said little about his two breakout roles while *All God's Chillun* and *The Emperor Jones* were running in the spring of 1924, he published an article in the African-American journal *Opportunity* the following December defending Harris, Jones, and their creator, Eugene O'Neill. "To have had the opportunity to appear in two of the finest plays of America's most distinguished playwright is good fortune that to me hardly seems credible," Robeson declared. To those blacks offended by O'Neill's failure to write a "truly heroic and noble role, one portraying the finest type of Negro," Robeson retorted, "I honestly believe that never will I portray a nobler type than Jim Harris or a more heroically tragic figure than Brutus Jones, excepting [William Shakespeare's] Othello."

By late 1924, thanks largely to his critically acclaimed portrayals of O'Neill's controversial protagonists Jim Harris and Brutus Jones, Robeson was making enough money from acting for Essie to resign from Presbyterian Hospital. From there on in, she intended to devote herself full time to managing his career, something that she had long wanted to do. Yet, even as "he increasingly viewed himself as an actor," Paul Robeson Jr. wrote, his father "also surveyed a wider world of options as a singer." During the second half of the 1920s, Robeson would establish himself not only as an internationally respected stage actor but also as an international concert and recording star, specializing in the beloved music of his youth—African-American spirituals and work songs.

5

International Stardom

Despite the critical acclaim that Paul Robeson received for his starring roles in *The Emperor Jones* and *All God's Chillun Got Wings* in the spring of 1924, he focused more on developing his musical abilities than his acting talents over the next several years. In November 1924, following a series of small, informal concerts in New York, Robeson gave his first professional concert at Copley Plaza in Boston. "The house was packed, the appreciative audience gave generous applause, and the critics were kind. Paul had confirmed that he had a potential concert career," Paul Robeson Jr. wrote. Robeson's singing career would not really take off until five months later, however, when he gave a groundbreaking concert in New York City with black pianist and arranger Lawrence "Larry" Brown, featuring only traditional African-American music.

TEAMING UP WITH LARRY BROWN

Robeson and Brown first met in London in the summer of 1922, when Robeson was touring England with *Voodoo*. Five years older than Robeson, Brown had also lost his mother as a young child. Unlike William Robeson, however, Brown's widowed father remarried, and Brown's supportive stepmother, Cenia, was destined to play an important role in his future career.

Convinced that Larry was musically gifted, Cenia scrimped and saved to pay for piano lessons for her stepson in their hometown of Jacksonville, Florida. After Brown graduated from high school, she encouraged him to move to Boston, where several top music conservatories were located. Having heard that employment opportunities for blacks were better in the North, he hoped to make enough money in Boston to cover his music school tuition. Instead, he discovered that, even in the North, most African Americans were relegated to menial, low-paying jobs. For four years, Brown worked as an elevator operator in a white residential hotel, shuttling tenants up and down the high-rise building. Finally, several of the hotel's well-to-do tenants, impressed by the young pianist's talent and determination, offered to pay Brown's tuition and living expenses so that he could study music full time. After Brown graduated from the New England Conservatory of Music in 1920, a local philanthropist gave him money to continue his musical instruction in London. By the time Robeson met him two years later, Brown had established himself in England as a skilled accompanist and arranger of music, especially African-American spirituals.

Brown and Robeson reconnected while Brown was visiting relatives in New York in early 1925. Robeson admired Brown's skillful arrangements of the traditional spirituals he had grown up singing and was eager to perform with him. Soon the two men were giving folk music recitals at the homes of friends, with Robeson singing and Brown accompanying him on the piano. Carl Van Vechten, an influential white writer and promoter of the Harlem Renaissance, was so impressed when Robeson and Brown performed at his house that he offered to help them arrange a public concert.

On April 19, 1925, Robeson and Brown presented their first public recital at the Provincetown Playhouse in Greenwich Village. Robeson's many prominent fans in New York, including Van Vechten and NAACP leader Walter White, heavily publicized the concert. By the night of the recital, every seat was sold out and hundreds of people had to be turned away at the door. The racially mixed audience, which included several New York music critics, was enthralled by Robeson and Brown's innovative program, which featured nothing but traditional African-American music. Martin Duberman observed:

> Robeson and Brown's concert marked the first time a black soloist . . . devoted an entire program to [African-American] spirituals and secular songs. Earlier, artists like [the black tenor] Roland Hayes had included one or two groups of Afro-American songs in a concert, but the music had been considered—by many blacks, too—as unsuited to a full evening's presentation because of its supposed monotony. Yet, as arranged by Larry Brown, . . . the actual range of the songs proved a revelation. . . . As one critic remarked with astonishment, the emotional stretch of the material included "infinite pathos, infinite gaiety, a sort of desperate wildness and an occasional majesty." Brown was praised for the skill of his arrangements, Robeson for the power of "a luscious, mellow bass-baritone," which lent the songs "an overwhelming inward conviction." . . . At the end of the concert, the reception was thunderous, with curtain calls and an additional sixteen encores following one after another.

A MUSICAL CAREER

The April 19 concert proved to be a major turning point for Robeson. Believing that he and Brown had been able to educate many of their white listeners—and black middle-class ones as well—regarding the musical sophistication and emotional power of African-American spirituals and work songs was enormously satisfying for Robeson. Moreover, the concert firmly established Robeson as a serious musical performer with broad appeal. Within weeks of the recital, Victor Records, one of the top American record labels, offered Robeson a lucrative contract. His early recordings for Victor of spirituals and other slave songs with Brown became instant hits, bringing Robeson numerous offers to sing on popular live radio broadcasts.

Soon after the Greenwich Village concert, Robeson and Brown signed a contract for their first American concert tour, scheduled to open in New York City. Beginning in January 1926 and running throughout the winter of 1926, Robeson and Brown gave a series of concerts of traditional African-American music at recital halls across the Northeast and the Midwest. They hoped that their concerts would help to overturn negative racial stereotypes regarding black culture by implanting in their racially mixed audiences "a new and better concept of the quality of our people's songs," as Robeson declared at a concert in Detroit on January 28. In the end, however, Robeson was deeply discouraged by his first concert tour. Although his singing received stellar reviews from local music critics, the recitals were poorly advertised, resulting in small audiences in most cities where Robeson performed. Another frustrating aspect of the tour for Robeson and Brown was securing acceptable accommodations, since many hotels did not want black guests. For example, when Robeson and Brown tried to check into their reserved rooms in Milwaukee, the hotel manager, who had been unaware of their skin color, told them that they would have to stay elsewhere because his other guests might object.

When Robeson and Brown refused to go quietly, the manager grudgingly honored their reservations but instructed them to use the hotel's side stairs rather than the main elevator.

With the tour's end in the spring of 1926, Robeson headed home to New York and immediately began rehearsals for a new theatrical production, *Black Boy*, about a prizefighter. Robeson hoped that his new role would help him recapture some of the momentum he had lost during his disappointing concert tour. Yet, while Robeson received glowing reviews for his acting and singing, critics panned the play's melodramatic script, and *Black Boy* closed after less than three weeks. In the wake of the play's failure, Essie Robeson threw together a second concert tour of the Northeast and Midwest with Brown for the winter and spring of 1927. Although hastily arranged, the new tour attracted more concertgoers than the first, probably because of the increasing popularity of Robeson's records and live radio broadcasts. Still, it brought in less money than Robeson had hoped. When Essie announced that she was pregnant with their first child shortly after the tour ended in May, Robeson fretted about his ability to support his growing family. Consequently, when he and Brown were approached that summer regarding a European concert tour, Robeson leapt at the opportunity.

FATHERHOOD AND A SHORT-LIVED EUROPEAN TOUR

In mid-October 1927, Robeson and Brown departed New York for Paris, the first stop on their tour. Robeson had visited Europe twice before: in 1922 with *Voodoo*, and in the fall of 1925 to act in a brief London run of *The Emperor Jones*. Robeson was delighted to have a chance to return to Europe, in large measure because he had encountered considerably less racial prejudice there than back home. Nonetheless, the timing of the tour was far from ideal. Now in the eighth month of her pregnancy, Essie had no choice but to remain in New York. Fortunately, Essie's mother, Eslanda Goode, volunteered to move in with her until after the baby arrived.

Paul Robeson perches his son, Paul Jr., on his shoulder as the latter arrived from the United States for a visit to England. At the time this photo was taken in April 1936, Paul Robeson had planned to have his son educated in England, where the entertainer was then living.

Robeson was gratified by the enthusiastic welcome he and Brown received in Paris, where they performed before standing-room audiences in some of the city's biggest concert halls. The quality and range of Robeson's bass-baritone voice and his magnetic stage presence thrilled Parisian critics and audiences alike.

On November 2, Robeson rejoiced when his mother-in-law cabled him that Essie had just delivered a healthy baby boy in a Brooklyn hospital. Soon after giving birth to Paul Jr. (or Pauli, as Essie called the baby), she developed several potentially dangerous health problems, including phlebitis—an inflammation of a vein. Determined to avoid upsetting her husband while he was on tour, Essie made no mention of her medical troubles in her letters to him in Paris. With Essie's health still showing no signs of improvement a full six weeks after Pauli's birth, Eslanda Goode finally took it upon herself to inform Robeson of his wife's true condition. Overwhelmed by guilt and worry, he immediately booked passage to New York. "It was so beautiful for you to let me go at the time of your childbirth," he wrote to Essie on Christmas Day from aboard the steamship *Mauretania*: "I'll never forget that—nor will I ever let you suffer again without my being around to help."

"OL' MAN RIVER"

By the late winter of 1928, things were looking up again for the Robesons. Essie had finally started to regain her strength, and Paul had won a part in a Broadway show, *Porgy*, about the residents of an impoverished fishing community in South Carolina. The play itself received generally poor reviews. But critics and audiences alike raved about Robeson's electrifying performance as a villainous stevedore (dockworker). After appearing in *Porgy* for a few weeks, he got an even better acting offer: He was asked to appear in a new London production of Oscar Hammerstein II and Jerome Kern's smash Broadway hit, *Show Boat.* He accepted immediately, and by early April, was on his way to

Paul Robeson, as seen starring in the 1936 film version of *Show Boat*. Robeson's performance of the musical's powerful ballad, "Ol' Man River," endeared him to audiences when he first performed it in the stage version.

London to begin rehearsals at the elegant Drury Lane Theatre. Essie was to follow him to London in May, leaving little Pauli in New York in the care of his grandmother, Eslanda Goode.

Based on a novel by Pulitzer Prize–winning author Edna Ferber, Hammerstein and Kern's classic musical focuses on the crew of a Mississippi River showboat during the late 1800s. One central plot line concerns an ill-fated interracial marriage between the boat's lead actor and actress, a biracial woman who had been passing for white. Joe, the character played by Robeson, was a stevedore on the Mississippi and, presumably, a former slave. Joe sings only one number in *Show Boat,* "Ol' Man River." But the hauntingly beautiful ballad, which Hammerstein and Kern reportedly composed with Robeson in mind, reappears throughout the musical in three separate refrains.

Robeson's powerful and unique interpretation of "Ol' Man River" was by far the most acclaimed feature of *Show Boat*'s long run at the Drury Lane Theater, which ultimately lasted for 350 performances. On May 4, the day after the musical opened, the theater critic for the *Morning Post* hailed Robeson's rendition of the Kern-Hammerstein song in the lavish production as "the thing that will be remembered first and last—the thing that held it all together." Hammerstein's lyrics for "Ol' Man River" provide a sympathetic portrayal of exploited black laborers struggling to survive in the brutally racist Deep South. Yet, while the "lyrics do include references to suffering and oppression," Sheila Tully Boyle and Andrew Bunie observed, "these are ripped from their historical context (institutionalized slavery) and further blunted by the repeated suggestion that some unnamed fate is responsible. The implication is that it is the destiny of the black man to suffer." Robeson, determined to reveal "the person beneath Joe's mask, a person who knew where he came from and who longed for freedom, completely altered the emphasis and direction of the song with his interpretation," Boyle and Bunie wrote, adding:

> What Robeson knew both emotionally and intellectually was that Joe's suffering was a product of the historical reality of slavery. . . . Robeson reconnected the song with its historical context by lingering over the lines dealing with oppression ("Body all *achin'* an' *racked* wid pain" and "*Bend* your knees/An' *bow* your head,/An' pull dat rope/Until you' *dead*") and giving the verbs special emphasis. . . . He sang slowly, reverently, and with great feeling the lines about the river Jordan, the only lines in the song suggesting Joe's longing for freedom:

"Let me go 'way from the Mississippi,
Let me go 'way from de white man boss,
Show me dat stream called de river Jordan,
Dat's de ol' stream dat I long to cross."

DID YOU KNOW?

From 1938 on, Paul Robeson began to perform his own modified version of the Jerome Kern–Oscar Hammerstein classic "Ol' Man River" at his concerts. Paul Robeson Jr. wrote in *The Undiscovered Paul Robeson* that his father's changes to the lyrics of the popular ballad transformed the song "from a submissive lament to a defiant rebuke." His new rendition of "Ol' Man River" was enormously popular with his concert audiences and quickly became his "artistic signature," according to Robeson Jr.:

Original Lyrics to "Ol' Man River" by Oscar Hammerstein II	Robeson's Version of "Ol' Man River"
Dere's an ol' man called de Mississippi;	*There's an ol' man called the Mississippi;*
Dat's de ol' man dat I'd like to be!	*That's the ol' man I don't like to be!*
What does he care if de world's got troubles?	*What does he care if the world's got troubles?*
What does he care if de land ain't free? . . .	*What does he care if the land ain't free . . .*
You an' me, we sweat an' strain,	*You an' me, we sweat an' strain,*
Body all achin' an' racked wid pain—Tote dat barge!	*Body all achin' an' racked wid pain—*
Lif' dat bale!	*Tote that barge and lif' that bale*
Git a little drunk,	*You show a little grit and*
An' you land in jail . . .	*You land in jail . . .*
Ah gits weary	*But I keeps laffin' instead of cryin'*
An' sick of tryin';	*I must keep fightin';*
Ah'm tired of livin'	*Until I'm dyin'*
An skeered of dyin',	*And Ol' Man River,*
But Ol' Man River,	*He just keeps rollin' along*
He jes' keeps rollin' along	

Many in Robeson's overwhelmingly white audiences were moved to tears by his interpretation of "Ol' Man River." Some Londoners went to the play over and over again just to hear him sing it. Boyle and Bunie asserted that Robeson "brought such power and dignity to this song, that no one who heard him ever forgot the experience. Once he had performed it, 'Ol' Man River' would be forever linked with Robeson's name."

LIFE IN LONDON

When *Show Boat* closed in March 1929 after a successful 10-month run, Robeson immediately began a concert tour of Central Europe with Larry Brown—their first continental tour since December 1927. In Vienna, Prague, and Budapest, Robeson—whose widely publicized role in *Show Boat* had turned him into a major international celebrity—drew

Troubled Marriage

While Paul Robeson was winning international acclaim as a singer and an actor during the late 1920s and early 1930s, his personal life was becoming increasingly strained. In the autumn of 1930, Essie published a controversial biography of her famous husband entitled *Paul Robeson, Negro*, which praised his talents as a performer but accused him of being neglectful of their son and unfaithful to her. Essie had written the biography in anger, after discovering a love letter to her husband from a young Englishwoman named Olivia Jackson. When Essie confronted him about the letter, he confessed to the affair and insisted that he loved Olivia and would continue to see her. In early 1932, Essie finally sued for divorce, and Robeson asked Jackson to marry him.

In September 1932, Robeson was devastated when Jackson, whose wealthy family objected to her marrying outside her race, abruptly ended their engagement. Soon after the breakup, he and Essie reconciled. But their marriage, though it would endure for another three decades until Essie's death in 1965, never fully recovered from his infidelity. "There was no going back, and they both realized that," Boyle and Bunie wrote. "The marriage had lost its romantic spark, and reconciliation would be, as [their friend] Dianne Loesser put it, 'amicable but not passionate.'"

packed houses and rave reviews. After returning to London in triumph, Robeson came close to selling out the Royal Albert Hall, the city's biggest concert auditorium, in late April. Robeson was the toast of England—adored by thousands of ordinary theater- and concertgoers as well as by the upper crust of London society.

Although Robeson returned to the United States for highly successful concert tours in late 1929 and early 1931, by the time *Show Boat* closed in March 1929, he and Essie decided to make England their home base, at least for the time being. While the Robesons did encounter some racial slights in Great Britain—including a well-publicized incident in which they were refused service at London's upscale Savoy Grill—the couple was welcome in most restaurants, hotels, theaters, and neighborhoods there, in sharp contrast to their experiences at home. By the end of 1929, the Robesons had moved Pauli and Eslanda Goode from New York to London and rented a large house in one of the city's most fashionable suburbs. There the Robesons threw elegant dinner parties with guest lists that included members of the British aristocracy and such American luminaries as dancer Fred Astaire and publishing magnate Alfred Knopf.

OTHELLO

In 1930, following well-received concert tours of the British Isles and Central Europe with Larry Brown, Robeson began rehearsals in London for the most important and challenging role of his acting career thus far: the lead role in William Shakespeare's play *Othello, the Moor of Venice.* One of Shakespeare's most acclaimed tragedies, *Othello* is set in sixteenth-century Venice and Cyprus. It tells the story of a noble Moorish general, who is duped by Iago, a villainous aide, into believing that his young Italian wife, Desdemona, has been unfaithful.

In the text of the play, Othello's race is ambiguous. He is referred to as a "Moor," a term used in Shakespeare's time to

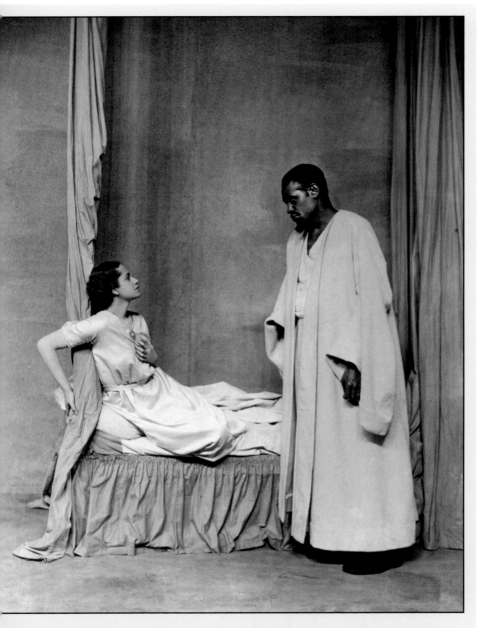

In 1930, Paul Robeson won great acclaim in London portraying the Moor of Venice in the Shakespeare's *Othello*, in which he played opposite Peggy Ashcroft, who took on the role of Desdemona, Othello's wife. Here, Othello and Desdemona are seen together in the famed bedchamber scene.

refer to dark-skinned people in general; today, the term refers to North Africans of Berber and Arab descent. Nonetheless, ever since *Othello* was first staged in London in 1604, white actors had almost always been cast in the title role. Not since the mid-1800s had a black man played Othello on the English stage. Consequently, Robeson's selection to play Othello in the new production received much attention from the press, particularly because at one point in the play, the general and his wife share a passionate kiss. Yet, in contrast to the uproar that surrounded the Provincetown Players' biracial production of *All God's Chillun Got Wings* in 1924, no serious threats were made against Robeson or his leading lady, British actress Peggy Ashcroft.

On May 19, 1930, *Othello* opened to a sellout audience at the Savoy Theatre. The night was a huge success for Robeson, with the audience giving him a standing ovation and 20 curtain calls. Reviews of his interpretation of Shakespeare's tragic hero, however, were mixed. Most critics showered Robeson with accolades for his portrayal, but some complained that he lacked the technical training and experience to do justice to such a complex role. In a May 24 article in the London *Sunday Times*, influential theater reviewer James Agate criticized Robeson for failing to give the Moorish general an air of authority.

> In the physical aspect Mr. Robeson largely failed. Though in the mere matter of inches he towered above everybody else, it was a tower which cringed. He walked with a stoop, his body sagged. . . . He did not trust his powers *as an actor* sufficiently; he certainly did not take the risk, with the result that all that Othello ought to be . . . , he was not.

Robeson himself would later dismiss his performance in *Othello* in 1930 as amateurish. Yet, when the production closed in July following a two-month run, Martin Duberman noted that Robeson told a newspaper reporter that "attempting the role . . . had nonetheless been liberating: 'Othello has taken away from me all kinds of fears, all sense of limitation. . . . Othello has opened to me new and wider fields; in a word, Othello has made me free.'"

6

New Interests, New Causes

As Robeson's performing career flourished during the early 1930s, he was flooded with well-paying offers. In 1932, he was awarded star billing in a lavish Broadway revival of *Show Boat* with a weekly salary of $1,500—an enormous sum for the time. Just as he had done four years earlier in London, Robeson thrilled his standing-room-only audiences with his rendition of "Ol' Man River." "Mr. Robeson has a touch of genius," Brooks Atkinson of the *New York Times* raved: "It is not merely his voice. . . . It is his understanding that gives 'Ol' Man River' an epic lift." In 1933, after giving a critically acclaimed performance in the first British production of *All God's Chillun Got Wings*, Robeson returned to the United States to star in his first "talkie," a film version of another Eugene O'Neill play with which he was closely associated, *The Emperor Jones*. Although some African-American reviewers panned the movie because

Dudley Digges *(left)* as Smithers and Paul Robeson as Emperor Brutus Jones are seen in the 1933 film *Emperor Jones*. It was one of the biggest film hits of Robeson's career.

they thought O'Neill's characterization of the greedy, self-made emperor, Brutus Jones, hurt the image of blacks, black and white moviegoers alike flocked to see Robeson's mesmerizing performance as the wily dictator.

A FASCINATION WITH AFRICA

Throughout his life, Robeson maintained his passion for learning. Even in the midst of an increasingly hectic performing schedule, Robeson took the time to pursue his intellectual interests, especially the folk cultures of other countries and ethnic groups. Sheila Tully Boyle and Andrew Bunie wrote: "He was passionately interested in discovering links between seemingly diverse cultures and told reporters he believed 'the best means of discovering [these] relationships . . . is through the sounds of their languages, their songs and their music.'" With that goal in mind, Robeson immersed himself in the study of foreign languages, including German, Chinese, Russian, French, Gaelic, Hebrew, and Yiddish (the language of Jews from Eastern and Central Europe) during the early 1930s. Soon, he began to add folk songs in these languages and others to his concert repertoires, to the delight of his audiences on both sides of the Atlantic.

In late 1933, Robeson enrolled at the London School of Oriental Languages to study African languages, including Swahili and Yoruba. At the same time, he learned everything he could about African history, art, and music. "Like most of Africa's children in America," Robeson later recalled in *Here I Stand*, "I had known little about the land of our fathers." The more he discovered about Africa's ancient civilization, the prouder he became of his ancestral homeland. "As I plunged, with excited interest, into my studies of Africa," Robeson wrote,

> I came to see that African culture was indeed a treasure-store for the world. Those who scorned the African languages as so many "barbarous dialects" could never know, of course, of the richness of those languages and of the great philosophy and epics of poetry that have come down through the ages in these ancient tongues.

Compelled "to speak out against the scorners," Robeson wrote articles about the glories of African culture, particularly its traditional music, for a number of British and American journals.

As part of his growing fascination with Africa, Robeson spent countless hours talking to African students attending universities and colleges in London. Most of the students' native lands had been gobbled up by the massive British Empire, which then controlled some 25 percent of the continent's population. Among Robeson's new African acquaintances were several young men who would eventually take leading roles in their peoples' struggles for self-rule during the 1950s and 1960s, including Jomo Kenyatta, who became Kenya's first president in 1964, a year after his country finally achieved independence from Great Britain. Under their influence, Robeson became an outspoken critic of British imperialism—and Western imperialism generally—in Africa. During the mid-1930s, Robeson also began to speak out against British rule in India after meeting the celebrated Indian nationalist leader, Jawaharlal Nehru, in London.

SANDERS OF THE RIVER

At a time when Africans were typically portrayed as buffoons or backward savages in plays and films, Robeson was eager to find acting projects that presented African culture in a more positive light. In 1934, Robeson thought he had found such a project when the respected British director Zoltan Korda asked him to star in his new film about Africa, *Sanders of the River*. Based on a popular story by the British novelist Edgar Wallace, the film script centered on the relationship between Sanders, a strong-willed British official in colonial Africa, and Bosambo, the resourceful tribal chieftain who faithfully supports him.

Robeson and the other lead actors shot all their scenes for *Sanders* on a London soundstage. Robeson was thrilled, however, that Korda intended to include highlights in the movie from the approximately 50,000 feet (15,240 meters) of film he had shot during a recent trip through Central Africa. From the start, Robeson had mixed feelings about the script. Although Bosambo was a man of considerable dignity and intelligence, Robeson was bothered by the fact that the chieftain invariably backed Sanders in the British official's ongoing struggle to maintain control over rebellious local tribes. Nonetheless, to Robeson, *Sanders* "represented indigenous African culture 'in a really magnificent way.'" The music, based on sound recordings Korda had made while touring Africa, "was excitingly authentic," Paul Robeson Jr. wrote. "Moreover, in a distinct advance beyond *The Emperor Jones, Sanders* . . . would permit him to play a hero who was entirely a 'good guy.'"

Sanders of the River premiered at London's Leicester Square Theatre on the evening of March 29, 1935, before a predominantly white audience. At the movie's conclusion, loud applause rocked the auditorium. When the crowd shouted for Robeson to come to the stage and sing, however, he uncharacteristically refused. Robeson had not had a chance to see the finished movie until that night, and he was disappointed by how it had turned out. Korda's use of authentic African footage, including traditional tribal rites and dances, pleased him a great deal. Robeson, though, was dismayed by what he saw as the film's pro-colonialist bias and demeaning characterization of Africans as either unruly savages or faithful servants to their white colonial "betters."

Although Korda's movie received mostly positive reviews in the London press, it caused an immediate uproar among anti-colonialists in England and Africa as well as among American civil rights leaders, such as writer and political activist Marcus Garvey. In the January 1936 edition of his magazine, *The Black Man*, Garvey scolded Robeson for appearing in what Garvey considered as an unabashedly racist film: "Paul Robeson ought to realize that the growing prejudice against Negroes in England . . . is due largely to the peculiar impression moving picture fans obtain from seeing such pictures." For the rest of his life, Robeson would be ashamed of his association with *Sanders of the River*. In an interview published in the *Pittsburgh*

(continues on page 68)

The Films of Paul Robeson

From 1924, when he made his first film, *Body and Soul*, through 1942, Paul Robeson appeared in a dozen motion pictures. Virtually all of the films were produced in England, Robeson's home base from the late 1920s until shortly after the outbreak of World War II in 1939. However, Robeson's most popular and well-known motion picture, *Show Boat* (1936), in which he reprised his stage role as the Mississippi stevedore Joe, was made in the United States by the leading Hollywood studio, Universal Pictures.

Besides *Sanders of the River*, Robeson starred in four other movies set in Africa during his nearly two-decade-long film career. In *Song of Freedom* (1936), he played a British opera singer who becomes the wise and benevolent ruler of an African island kingdom after traveling there to learn more about his cultural and family roots. In sharp contrast to his embarrassment over *Sanders*, Robeson was proud of *Song of Freedom*, and particularly of the glowing reviews the movie received in the African-American press for its positive images of black people. One year after making *Song of Freedom*, Robeson starred in *Jericho*, about an American soldier who stays in North Africa following World War I (1914–1918) and becomes a respected physician and tribal leader. Many of Robeson's scenes were shot on location in Egypt, giving him the opportunity to visit the African continent for the first time. Surprisingly, Robeson never returned to Africa, although he remained an outspoken champion of African independence throughout his life, serving for nearly two decades as chairman of the Council on African Affairs, an anticolonialist organization he helped found in 1937.

In 1939, Robeson made what he would later identify as his favorite film, *Proud Valley*, about a heroic black coal miner in Wales, a country that is part of the United Kingdom. Written by Herbert Marshall, a friend of Robeson's with ties to the British labor movement, *Proud Valley* provided a gripping portrait of Wales's poverty-stricken and exploited mine workers. Shortly before Robeson completed *Proud Valley*, World War II erupted in Europe, and Robeson decided to move his family from London to the United States.

After turning down several lucrative offers to appear in Hollywood films because he thought that the scripts perpetuated black stereotypes, he agreed

(continues)

(opposite page) Here, Paul Robeson appears on a poster for the 1936 film *Song of Freedom*. Robeson was particularly proud of his work in this groundbreaking movie.

(continued)

to play a poor Southern sharecropper in *Tales of Manhattan* for Twentieth Century Fox in 1941. Robeson hoped the movie would help educate white audiences about the hardships and injustices endured by Southern blacks under the sharecropping system. When he saw the final cut of *Tales of Manhattan*, however, Robeson was appalled. Most of the film's black characters mirrored old Hollywood stereotypes of African Americans as childlike and gullible. Shortly after Twentieth Century Fox released *Tales of Manhattan* in 1942, Robeson announced that he was through with Hollywood because of the demeaning way in which the American movie industry portrayed blacks. After his disappointing experience with *Tales of Manhattan*, he never accepted another acting role in a motion picture—British or American—for the rest of his professional career.

(continued from page 65)

Courier on August 13, 1949, nearly 15 years after the film was released, Robeson said he had donated every cent he earned from the movie to charity: "I hate the picture. I have tried to buy it, but because it is a tremendous money-maker, have not been able to do so. . . . I committed a faux pas [blunder] which, when viewed in retrospect, convinced me I had failed to weigh the problems of 150,000,000 native Africans."

DISCOVERING THE SOVIET UNION

In late 1934, Paul and Essie Robeson made what would turn out to be a life-changing trip to the Union of Soviet Socialist Republics (USSR). Robeson had never visited the Soviet Union before, but he had heard glowing reports about the communist nation from Essie's brothers, Frank and John Goode, who had moved there in search of better employment opportunities. (Like socialism, communism calls for public ownership of all land, factories, and other economic

In the 1930s, Paul Robeson came to believe that the Soviet Union was a freer and more just society than the United States. Here, the Soviet dictator Joseph Stalin *(third from right, upper stand)* is shown on November 17, 1936, reviewing Soviet army forces during the nineteenth anniversary of the Bolshevik Revolution. The other government officials pictured *(left to right, upper stand)* are Ivan Mezhlauk, Nikita Khrushchev, Aleksandr Chubar, Andrei Andreyev, Yan Rudzutak, Vyacheslav Molotov, Stalin, Lazar Kaganovich, and Mikhail Kalinin.

resources. In keeping with the teachings of Russia's first communist leader, Vladimir I. Lenin, the Soviets also insisted that only a tightly disciplined revolutionary vanguard, in the form of the Communist Party, could defend their state from capitalist influences.) Besides spending time with his brothers-in-law in Moscow, Robeson planned to meet with the renowned

Russian filmmaker Sergei Eisenstein to discuss a movie Eisenstein wanted to make with him about the Haitian revolutionary Toussaint L'Ouverture.

High-ranking Communist Party officials and ordinary Soviet citizens alike enthusiastically welcomed Robeson during his two-week stay in the USSR. Robeson marveled at the seeming lack of racial prejudice among the Russian people. "I was not prepared for the endless friendliness, which surrounded me from the moment I crossed the border," he told a reporter for the left-wing journal, the *Daily Worker*, after returning to London in January 1935. "I was rested and buoyed up by the lovely, honest, wondering looks which did not see a 'Negro.' When these people looked at me, they were just happy and interested. There were no 'double looks,' no venom, no superiority. . . . In Soviet Russia, I breathe freely for the first time in my life." Robeson was also impressed by the Communist leadership's apparent commitment to achieving complete equality among the many population groups that inhabited the massive country. Soviet lawmakers had even gone so far as to prohibit all forms of racial, ethnic, or gender discrimination in the USSR's constitution, he noted approvingly.

Following a second, equally gratifying trip to Moscow in 1936, Robeson decided to send nine-year-old Pauli to school in the Soviet Union, the one country in which he believed his son could grow up completely free of racism. During the fall and early winter of 1936–1937, Robeson made his first concert tour of the USSR after settling Pauli at his new school in Moscow. Robeson, who was fluent in Russian by this time, added a number of Russian folk songs to his concert repertoire, and the tour was a resounding success. Six months later, he and Essie returned to the USSR to spend the summer with Pauli in a resort town near the Caucasus Mountains, in what would be Robeson's last trip to the Soviet Union until after World War II (1939–1945).

During their long family vacation, Robeson pressed Pauli to tell him all about his time in Moscow, including anything he might have heard from his classmates regarding some disturbing reports about recent political developments in the Soviet Union. Over the previous year, Joseph Stalin, Russia's dictatorial leader since the late 1920s, had overseen a series of purges of Communist and military officials whom he viewed as potential threats to his totalitarian rule. The highly publicized purges, which had left at least 400,000 dead and hundreds of thousands more imprisoned in forced labor camps by the end of 1937, were critical to Russia's national security and the continued success of its communist revolution, Stalin declared. According to Stalin, saboteurs and spies working for Nazi Germany's fascist leader, Adolf Hitler, and his virulently anti-communist regime in Berlin, had infiltrated the Soviet government and military. (Fascism is a system of government typically marked by strict economic and social control; a strong, centralized government headed by a dictator; and an official policy of extreme racism and nationalism.)

What Robeson thought about Stalin's brutal purges is unknown, since he never spoke about them in public. He was sufficiently shaken by Pauli's stories of schoolmates whose relatives had been imprisoned or simply vanished without warning, however, to send his son back to England for the next school year. Nonetheless, Robeson's fundamental faith in the superiority of the Soviet system, with its emphasis on social and racial equality, remained firm. In the fall of 1937, he received special permission from Moscow to enroll Pauli at a Soviet-run school in London for the children of Russian diplomats.

FIGHTING FASCISM

Despite any private concerns he might have had regarding the excesses of Stalin's iron-fisted rule, Robeson was convinced that Stalin and the rest of the USSR's Communist leadership were sincerely devoted to building a more just society that was free from prejudice. At the same time, Robeson saw the Soviet Union as the world's only reliable bulwark against the recent spread of fascism in Europe, a turn of events he found deeply troubling. By the mid-1930s, fascist dictators controlled Italy and Germany, fascist ideas were gaining popularity in France, and Spain was embroiled in a bloody civil war pitting right-wing insurgents under the fascist general Francisco Franco against the country's democratically elected, socialist government. Hitler and Italy's fascist leader, Benito Mussolini, supported Franco's Nationalist Army, while the Soviet Union was providing military aid to the Spanish government's Republican forces. Robeson had become a committed anti-fascist during his first trip to the Soviet Union in 1934, when he and Essie had a 24-hour layover in Berlin. Robeson found his brief stay in Nazi Germany extremely stressful—at one point he even feared that a group of Hitler's virulently racist storm troopers, or "brown

IN HIS OWN WORDS...

Speaking at a rally in London on June 24, 1937, to aid the victims of the Spanish Civil War, Paul Robeson explained what he viewed as the artist's moral duty to take a stand on the pressing social and political issues of the day:

The challenge must be taken up. . . . The artist must elect to fight for freedom or slavery. I have made my choice, I had no alternative. The history of the capitalist era is characterized by the degradation of my people. Despoiled of their lands, their culture destroyed, they are . . . denied equal opportunity of the law and deprived of their rightful place in the respect of their fellows. . . .

Not through blind faith or coercion, but conscious of my course, I take my place with you. I stand with you in unalterable support of the Government of Spain, duly and regularly chosen by its lawful sons and daughters.

shirts," patrolling the Berlin train station intended to lynch him. "Really, it was like seeing the Ku Klux Klan in power," he later told his friend and biographer, Lloyd Brown. "Brown shirts instead of white sheets, but the same idea."

During the summer of 1937, Franco's Nationalists, backed by their fascist allies in Germany and Italy, intensified their military campaign to overthrow Spain's elected government. With the situation looking increasingly grim for the Republican Army, and the anti-fascist cause in Europe in general, Robeson reached a defining moment in his life. From there on in, he decided, his performing career and his personal life must take second place to his political and social activism. Interrupting his vacation with Pauli and Essie in Russia, Robeson flew to London on June 24 to sing and speak at a large fundraising rally at Royal Albert Hall for Spanish refugee children. In an often quoted speech, Robeson spoke eloquently of the artist's responsibility to use his talents and influence to help win freedom and social equality for all people, including not only the victims of fascist tyranny in Spain, but also those of racism and economic exploitation worldwide.

In January 1938, at great risk to his safety, Robeson traveled to war-torn Spain to perform for the beleaguered Republican Army and demonstrate his solidarity with its cause. During an emotional weeklong concert tour, Robeson sang and offered words of encouragement to the governmental troops and the tens of thousands of volunteers, many of them members of European or American left-wing political or labor organizations, who flocked to Spain to aid the Republican forces. Despite their courageous efforts, however, Franco's forces, with the invaluable assistance of fascist Germany and Italy, were in firm control of Spain by the summer of 1939. By this time as well, Hitler, taking advantage of the reluctance of the other major European powers to forcibly halt Nazi aggression, had annexed Austria and Czechoslovakia.

After Nazi troops invaded Poland on September 1, Britain and France finally declared war on Germany on September 3, 1939, launching World War II in Europe. A month later, after Robeson finished filming what would turn out to be his last British film, *Proud Valley*, he and his family left England for New York. Back in his homeland, Robeson planned to continue using his artistic gifts and celebrity not only to help stop fascism in Europe, but to fight all forms of racial, economic, and political oppression in the United States and around the globe.

7

Robeson Becomes Controversial

Shortly after returning to the United States in October 1939, Robeson made what would turn out to be one of the wisest decisions of his career when he agreed to perform a patriotic song entitled "Ballad for Americans" for a popular CBS radio program. Robeson's stirring rendition of the 11-minute ballad, which celebrated America's historic commitment to democratic ideals, was a huge hit with listeners around the country. The broadcast created such a sensation that CBS executives asked Robeson to repeat it on New Year's Day 1940. A few weeks later, he recorded the song for Victor Records. Throughout 1940, Robeson sang "Ballad" for sold-out audiences across the United States, including a historic performance in July at the Hollywood Bowl before 30,000 fans, the biggest crowd ever to attend an event at the famed Los Angeles amphitheater.

Paul Robeson sings on CBS Radio in 1939. His powerful performance of the patriotic song "Ballad for Americans" was enormously popular with listeners across the country.

Over the next few years, Robeson's popularity would soar to unprecedented heights in his American homeland. By 1942, he was the highest paid concert artist in the United States. The following year, Robeson's reputation as America's foremost black performer was cemented when he starred in an acclaimed Broadway production of *Othello* that ran for 296 shows, a record for a Shakespearean production on Broadway.

FIGHTING OPPRESSION OVERSEAS AND AT HOME

As Robeson's performing career in the United States was blossoming during the first half of the 1940s, he somehow found the time in his hectic schedule of concert tours, recording sessions, and theater productions to sing and speak for a variety of civil rights, humanitarian, and labor organizations. From December 1941, when the United States entered World War II following the Japanese attack on Pearl Harbor, until the war's end in September 1945, Robeson also generously volunteered his time and talents to the cause of defeating the fascist regimes of Germany and Italy and their ally, Japan. He performed at dozens of war bond rallies and war-relief fundraisers across the country, often giving impassioned speeches on the evils of fascism between musical numbers. In 1945, he put his career on hold for more than two months to entertain American troops in Europe as part of the United Service Organizations (USO), a nonprofit group that provides recreational and morale services to U.S. military members. The European tour, which also featured Robeson's longtime accompanist, Larry Brown, was the USO's first overseas interracial tour since the organization's founding four years earlier. Robeson's tireless wartime volunteering did not go unnoticed in Washington. Several high-ranking government officials, including the secretary of the treasury and the secretary of war (as the secretary of defense was then called), and First Lady Eleanor Roosevelt, made a point of publicly thanking him for his many contributions to the American war effort.

During the war years, Robeson was not only concerned with defending democracy abroad by helping to defeat the forces of fascism in Europe and Japanese imperialism in East Asia. He was also deeply concerned about expanding democracy at home by championing the rights of workers, especially the heavily exploited black labor force. Robeson had first become interested in labor issues when he was living in Europe. In Great Britain, he befriended the top leaders of the British Labor Party as well as many ordinary workers, including African stevedores toiling for starvation wages on London's docks and Welsh miners enduring dangerous conditions in the country's coal mines. Based on his experiences in Great Britain, Robeson decided that organizing was the first step for workers of all races and nationalities in achieving a better life. Consequently, when he returned to the United States in late 1939, he volunteered to help the Congress of Industrial Organizations (CIO) to recruit new members, especially among the African-American community. Founded in 1932, the CIO was a federation of interracial industrial and craft unions in the United States and Canada; in 1955, it merged with the American Federation of Labor (AFL) to form the AFL-CIO.

Robeson's commitment to bettering the lives of struggling workers in the United States and throughout the world was closely linked to his growing faith in socialism as the most just existing system of government. Leftist friends in the British labor movement had first kindled Robeson's interest in socialism and communism, an interest that was greatly strengthened by his visit to the Soviet Union in 1934. Communism, or Marxism, is based on the teachings and writings of the nineteenth-century German writer and revolutionary Karl Marx, who described his beliefs in *The Communist Manifesto,* a book coauthored with Friedrich Engels and published in 1848.

Playing Othello on Broadway

Produced by the New York-based theatrical society, the Theatre Guild, the groundbreaking Broadway production of *Othello, the Moor of Venice* starring Paul Robeson opened on October 19, 1943. Destined to be the longest-running Shakespearean play on Broadway, the production marked the first time a black man had interpreted the role of Othello in a mainstream theatrical production in the United States. Directed by one of the United States' first prominent female directors, Margaret Webster, and costarring the respected stage actress Uta Hagen, the Theatre Guild's production was ecstatically received by New York audiences and critics alike. Much of the positive attention focused on Robeson and his mesmerizing performance as the Moorish general who murders his young Venetian wife, Desdemona, after being tricked into believing she had been unfaithful.

When the final curtain came down on *Othello*'s opening night, the ovation for Robeson lasted a full 20 minutes, one of the longest in the history of Broadway. Most reviewers wholeheartedly agreed with the audience's glowing assessment of Robeson's performance. One leading drama critic even called it the most notable interpretation of Shakespeare's tragic hero of the entire century. In developing his nontraditional interpretation of the role for the Broadway production, Robeson downplayed jealous rage as a motive for Othello's murder of Desdemona, focusing instead on the general's powerful sense of personal honor and pride in his racial and cultural heritage. As Robeson explained years later to a concert audience in New York's Carnegie Hall, from his point of view, Othello did not kill Desdemona from "savage passion. No. Othello came from a culture as great as that of ancient Venice. He came from an Africa of equal stature, and he felt he was betrayed. He felt his honor was betrayed, and his human dignity was betrayed."

The impact of Robeson's interpretation of Othello in the early 1940s, at a time when blacks were still typically portrayed in films and onstage as naïve, overemotional, and childlike, was immense. In 1956, the distinguished African-American actor James Earl Jones, who was about to tackle the role of Othello himself for the first time that year, remembered the effect Robeson's performance had on him when he saw the Broadway production as a teenager: "[I]t was essentially a message he gave out: 'Don't play me cheap. Don't *anybody* play me cheap.' And he reached way beyond arrogance . . . way beyond that. Just by his presence, he commanded that nobody play him cheap. And that was astounding to see in 1943."

According to Marx and Engels, the capitalist system will eventually die out, and the proletariat (or lower working class) will ultimately create a completely stateless and classless society in which the decisions of the nation are made in the best interests of the collective society as a whole. The first step on this road to communism would be socialism, in which the workers, rather than a few wealthy elites, control all factories, land, and other means of production.

Robeson was particularly hopeful that socialism, with its emphasis on the solidarity (unity) and fundamental rights of the working man and woman, would provide the means by which blacks could finally become full and equal members of American society. After moving back to the United States, Robeson vowed to make achieving full civil rights for America's impoverished and downtrodden black population a central focus of his life and work. To that end, Robeson began to refuse to sing or act at segregated theaters, where blacks and whites had to sit separately, and campaigned for the integration of Major League Baseball, which finally occurred in 1947.

Perhaps no other civil rights issue was more important to Robeson than fighting racially motivated violence, however. Following an alarming rise in lynchings of blacks in the South in 1945 and 1946, Robeson helped organize the American Crusade to End Lynching (ACEL). In June 1946, he led an interracial delegation to the White House to ask President Harry Truman—who would desegregate the armed forces by executive order in 1948—to support a federal antilynching bill. To Robeson's disgust, Truman, concerned about his political standing among white Southerners, many of whom opposed an antilynching bill, turned down the ACEL's request.

ROBESON'S CONTROVERSIAL STAND ON THE USSR

During World War II, Robeson helped raise thousands of dollars for Russian war relief and often praised the Soviets at his concerts and other public appearances for what he saw as their devotion to social and racial equality. Although the United States and the Soviet Union would become allies during the war, the U.S. government as well as many ordinary Americans had been wary of Russia's totalitarian regime ever since the Communists first seized power in 1917. But when Hitler, despite signing a non-aggression pact with Stalin two years earlier, suddenly invaded the USSR in June 1941, American attitudes toward the communist country softened. The Soviet Union, which played a decisive role in the ultimate defeat of Nazi Germany, suffered enormous losses during World War II, including the deaths of an estimated 25 million soldiers and civilians and the destruction of thousands of cities and towns. Consequently, although Robeson's outspoken admiration for the Soviet regime alarmed the FBI's staunchly anti-communist director, J. Edgar Hoover, it did not hurt his standing among the American public.

Soon after Hitler's defeat in 1945, however, suspicion toward the USSR and its Communist leadership began to build again among Americans. Fueled by the Soviet takeover of Eastern Europe after World War II and the testing of the first Russian atomic bomb in August 1949, anti-communist paranoia reached new heights in the United States during the second half of the 1940s. The Cold War (1945–1991), pitting the United States and its Western allies against the Soviet Union and its Eastern European satellites, had begun. The intense economic, military, and political competition between the United States and the Soviet Union that marked the Cold War years never resulted in a full-scale war between the two superpowers. But during the first decade of the Cold War, many Americans feared that the Soviets sought nothing less than world domination and that a nuclear showdown with the USSR was all but inevitable. Egged on by such rabidly anti-communist politicians as Senator Joseph

In May 1948, Paul Robeson tells the Senate Judiciary Committee that he is willing to go to jail rather than answers questions about whether or not he is a communist.

McCarthy, many Americans also feared communist subversion in their homeland. Greatly adding to this paranoia, the House Committee on Un-American Activities and the Senate Permanent Subcommittee on Investigations, with which McCarthy was closely linked, devoted themselves to rooting out communist agents and sympathizers in the American government, military, and entertainment industry from 1945 through much of the 1950s.

The escalating anti-Soviet sentiment in the United States appalled Robeson. From the start, he made up his mind that McCarthy or the other communist-witch-hunters would not intimidate him. Consequently, when Robeson was ordered to appear before the California State Legislature's Committee on Un-American Activities in October 1946 to discuss his alleged ties to the Communist Party of the United States, he boldly praised the Soviet Union's commitment to true democracy. Although he denied being a member of the

DID YOU KNOW?

By 1948, Paul Robeson was thoroughly disgusted with both the Republican and the Democratic parties because of their failure to take a firm stand against lynching and segregation and their strong anti-Soviet rhetoric. He gained a renewed sense of hope for the American political process, however, when Henry A. Wallace, a former secretary of agriculture and vice president under Franklin Roosevelt, agreed to run for president under the banner of the newly created Progressive Party. The Progressive platform embraced causes dear to Robeson's heart, including full civil rights for Americans of all races, labor rights, and improved relations with the Soviet Union. Although Wallace was not a communist himself, his candidacy was officially endorsed by the Communist Party of the United States, a major target of the House Committee on Un-American Activities and the FBI's vehemently anti-communist director, J. Edgar Hoover.

Robeson spent countless hours stumping for Wallace, with undercover FBI agents shadowing him everywhere he went at Hoover's personal behest. Robeson campaigned heavily for Wallace in the South, where he received numerous death threats from the Ku Klux Klan. In the November elections, Wallace received just over one million votes, far fewer than the victorious Democratic incumbent, Harry Truman, or the Republican candidate, Thomas E. Dewey. Despite the Progressive Party's disappointing showing at the polls, however, Robeson took comfort from the fact that Wallace's challenge from the left prodded President Truman into making some concessions to the civil rights movement, including a pledge to desegregate the armed forces.

Paul Robeson and former Vice President Henry A. Wallace are shown at Chicago Stadium on May 14, 1947, where both addressed the audience. In 1948, Robeson endorsed Wallace's run for the presidency at the head of the ticket of the newly created Progressive Party.

Communist Party, he told his interrogators that he could "just as conceivably join the Communist Party, more so today, than I could join the Republican or Democratic Party." Robeson also continued to express admiration for the USSR at his concerts and other public appearances. Convinced that reports of Russian tyranny in Eastern Europe and a new round of bloody Stalinist purges inside the USSR were propaganda lies, Robeson insisted that the Soviet system provided a model of social and economic justice for the rest of the world to follow.

By the late 1940s, Robeson was paying a high price for his outspokenness. Frequently denounced in newspaper editorials and radio commentaries for his "communist sympathies," Robeson found himself shunned by former fans and barred from concert halls in towns and cities across America. FBI agents went so far as to pressure recording studio and auditorium managers not to rent out their facilities to Robeson. Although he stayed busy performing at union events, colleges, and African-American churches, Robeson's income had fallen dramatically by 1949. That winter he traveled to the British Isles, where he remained popular and knew he could still find regular concert work. After performing at packed concert halls for two months, Robeson decided to take a short break from his British tour to attend the World Peace Congress in Paris in April 1949. It would turn out to be a fateful decision.

PARIS AND MOSCOW

The World Peace Congress of April 1949 brought together nearly 2,000 peace activists from 50 countries, many of whom had ties to left-wing organizations or causes. On April 20, Robeson was asked to give a short speech to the delegates. In the speech, he blasted anti-Soviet hysteria in the United States for diverting the government's attention and resources away from urgent issues at home, particularly achieving full civil rights for blacks and a better life for all workers:

> We in America do not forget that it was on the backs of the white workers from Europe and on the backs of millions of blacks that the wealth of America was built. And we are resolved to share it equally. We reject any hysterical raving that urges us to make war on anyone. Our will to fight for peace is strong.

> We shall not make war on anyone. We shall not make war
> on the Soviet Union. . . . We shall support peace and friend-
> ship among all nations. . . .

Immediately after Robeson finished speaking, a reporter for the Associated Press (AP) wired a dispatch back to the United States that supposedly quoted directly from his speech. In truth, large portions of the dispatch were made up. According to the fabricated news bulletin, Robeson declared that it was "unthinkable that American Negroes would go to war on behalf of those who have oppressed us for generations against the Soviet Union, which in one generation has raised our people to the full dignity of mankind."

In response to the AP dispatch, newspaper headlines across the United States blared that Robeson was telling African Americans not to fight for their country. As the outcry against Robeson grew over the following days, many of his former allies, including a number of CIO leaders, publicly rebuked him for his Paris speech. Because the AP dispatch made it look as if Robeson was speaking for all African Americans, some prominent black civil rights leaders, including Roy Wilkins of the NAACP, also felt compelled to denounce his apparently treasonous remarks. Just three years earlier the NAACP had presented Robeson with its highest award, the Spingarn Medal, for his many professional and civic contributions. Robeson did not help matters by failing to refute the fabricated AP bulletin. When hostile American reporters hounded him with questions as he was leaving Paris a few days after the speech about whether he felt a deeper loyalty to the USSR than he did to his birth country, Robeson lost his temper, instead of explaining that he had been misquoted. "Why should Negroes ever fight against the only nation in the world where racial discrimination is prohibited and where people live freely?" he shot back.

Robeson's popularity among the American press and public plummeted further after he decided to visit Moscow in early June 1949, before returning home to New York. The visit started out well: Robeson was thrilled to be back in Moscow after more than 10 years, and the Soviets were as welcoming as ever. Robeson, however, soon began to notice something troubling. He and Essie had made many Jewish Russian friends over the years, including several prominent film directors and writers, yet not one of them was present at any of the state or social functions he attended.

Rumors that Stalin had recently begun a brutal anti-Semitic purge had been rife in Western Europe, and Robeson was clearly suspicious. On his previous visits to the USSR, he and Essie had become especially close to the Jewish poet Itzik Feffer. Now he demanded to meet with him. At first, Soviet officials said Feffer was away on vacation and could not be reached. But when Robeson refused to back down, Feffer finally appeared at Robeson's Moscow hotel room. Communicating with notes and hand gestures, Feffer let Robeson know that the room was bugged and that he had been in prison for the last seven months and fully expected to be executed. He also indicated that Stalin's henchmen had killed their mutual friend, the Jewish director Solomon Mikhoels. (Just as he had predicted, Feffer was executed as well in 1952.)

A few days after his visit with Feffer, Robeson gave a concert at Moscow's Tchaikovsky Hall. At the end of the concert, Robeson daringly paid tribute to Feffer and Mikhoels by performing "Song of the Warsaw Ghetto Rebellion," the anthem of the Polish Jews who courageously fought the Nazi army in 1943. Stalin was undoubtedly displeased by Robeson's thinly veiled attack on his anti-Semitic campaign. He must have been relieved, however, when Robeson had only praise for the Soviet Union on his return to the United States in mid-June. That Robeson never revealed what he knew about

Stalin's deadly purge, even when reporters questioned him directly about it, remains difficult to understand for Robeson scholars. But Robeson seems to have convinced himself that, whatever moral defects Stalin might possess, the Soviet economic and social system still provided the greatest hope for the world's oppressed, including American blacks suffering from racial discrimination and millions of Africans chafing under colonial rule.

PEEKSKILL AND ITS AFTERMATH

In late August 1949, a little more than two months after Robeson flew back to New York from Moscow, his unpopularity at home exploded into violence. On August 27, he was scheduled to perform at an outdoor concert at a picnic ground near Peekskill, in Westchester County, New York. The event was being held to benefit the Harlem chapter of the Civil Rights Congress (CRC), a left-leaning civil rights group that its conservative critics accused of being a communist front organization. (A front organization is a body that is set up and dominated by another organization.) The concert was canceled at the last minute, however, when a mob of white protesters began to hurl rocks and racial epithets at Robeson's racially mixed audience as they tried to enter the picnic ground. Later, some anti-Robeson protesters made a bonfire of concert programs and camp chairs and set a Ku Klux Klan–style cross on fire. Declaring that "my people and I won't be frightened by crosses burning in Peekskill or anywhere else," Robeson defiantly rescheduled the concert for September 4. It was to be held at a long unused golf course, close to the site of the canceled concert.

When the CRC put out a request for volunteers to guard Robeson at the September 4 concert, the Fur and Leather Workers Union and several other leftist and multiracial unions immediately responded. Worried citizens of Peekskill also persuaded Governor Thomas E. Dewey of New York to call in hundreds of state troopers and local deputy sheriffs to help keep the peace. The concert itself went forward without a hitch. Surrounded by a phalanx of burly trade union security guards, Robeson performed for 15,000 appreciative fans and CRC members from a makeshift stage atop a sound truck. But when the mixed race audience started to leave the golf course, they found themselves driving through a gantlet of rock- and brick-throwing protesters, many shouting racial slurs about blacks and Jews. By the end of the evening, nearly 150 concertgoers, including a number of women and children, had been injured, some of them seriously. According to eyewitness accounts, the state troopers made little or no effort to intervene on behalf of the terrorized audience members, and a few local deputy sheriffs actually helped rioters drag concertgoers out of their cars and beat them.

Robeson was saddened and disgusted by the Peekskill riots, which he denounced as "fascist." On October 12, 1949, he sent an open letter to President Truman asking him to order a full investigation of the brutal attacks and "those who conspired, connived, and assisted" in them. "The warning is clear, Mr. President," Robeson wrote.

> The Peekskill outrages are the product of that perverted Americanism which brands as unAmerican those who speak out for peace, who stand up for their constitutional rights and those of their fellow-men.... Peekskill was a reminder of Hitlerite Germany where fascism got its start with organized mob assaults, with official sanction, against the Jewish people, in the name of German "patriotism" and "anti-Communism."

While a federal investigation of the Peekskill riot never took place, Westchester County officials did order a grand jury investigation of the events of September 4. Its report exonerated the state troopers and local deputy sheriffs of charges that they had neglected to perform their duties and concluded that the concert's "communist" organizers had deliberately provoked the riot for propaganda purposes.

Once again, however, Robeson refused to be intimidated. On November 10, 1949, he daringly appeared as the main speaker at a banquet in New York City sponsored by the National Council of Soviet-American Friendship. "We anti-fascists—the true lovers of American democracy—have a tremendous responsibility," he told his audience. "If we mobilize with courage, the forces of world fascism will be defeated—in Europe, in Africa, and in the United States."

8

Last Years and Legacy

Anti-Communist sentiment in the United States reached new heights following the outbreak of the Korean War on June 25, 1950. The war, which lasted for three years, began when communist North Korea, a close ally of the USSR, invaded anti-communist and pro-Western South Korea. Shortly after the invasion, President Truman announced that he was sending U.S. troops to South Korea to help defend its freedom under the banner of the United Nations, the international peacekeeping organization. Robeson reacted angrily to Truman's commitment of American forces to the Asian conflict, even though most Americans supported the president. At a civil rights rally in Madison Square Garden in New York on June 28, Robeson denounced Truman's decision to send American troops to Korea. Then, referring to his controversial remarks a year earlier about African Americans and the USSR, he declared: "I have said it before and say it again, that the place for the Negro people to fight for their freedom is here at home."

AN EXILE IN HIS OWN LAND

A month after Robeson's inflammatory Madison Square Garden speech, the State Department informed the entertainer that it was canceling his passport. The only reason the State Department gave for this extraordinary action was that it "would not be in the best interests of the United States" for Robeson to travel abroad. Robeson immediately filed a civil lawsuit to get his passport reinstated, declaring that he needed to travel abroad to support himself financially. There was a great deal of truth to his claim. In the wake of the Peekskill riot and the outbreak of the Korean War, Robeson was not only banned from theater and concert stages across the country but also from American radio and television. Record stores even removed his records from their shelves.

Letters demanding the return of Robeson's passport poured into the State Department from around the globe. Nonetheless, in 1951, a federal judge upheld the right of the department to restrict Robeson's travel. Robeson could only have his passport back, State Department officials told him, if he signed a pledge saying he would refrain from giving any political speeches while he was out of the country. Insisting that as an American citizen he had the constitutional right to travel and speak freely, Robeson instructed his lawyers to keep fighting.

In the end, Robeson's legal battle with the State Department dragged on for another seven years before his passport was returned. Although the boycott of Robeson by the American entertainment world remained firmly in place throughout this period, Robeson still found plenty to occupy his time. He studied music and world culture; chaired an anticolonial organization, the Council on African Affairs; wrote a regular column for *Freedom*, a left-leaning civil rights publication he started with W.E.B. Du Bois; spoke at leftist union rallies;

and performed at African-American churches, particularly in Harlem, where he made his home.

As the civil rights movement gained momentum in the mid-1950s, Robeson also became increasingly militant in his demands for black pride and in African Americans' cultural, political, and economic self-sufficiency. In this regard, Robeson

IN HIS OWN WORDS...

In 1958, Robeson's book, *Here I Stand*, was published by Othello Associates, a small publishing company based in Harlem. The book was favorably reviewed by the African-American press but totally ignored by the mainstream American press until the 1970s. Although often labeled as an autobiography, only the first chapter of *Here I Stand*, which describes Robeson's childhood and adolescence, is actually autobiographical. The rest focuses on Robeson's social and political beliefs. Much of the volume is concerned with the then-budding civil rights movement, aimed at ending segregation and securing equal civil rights for African Americans. In his book, Robeson called on his fellow African Americans to fight for their freedom:

> As I see it, the challenge which today confronts the Negro people in the United States can be stated in two propositions:
>
> 1. Freedom can be ours, here and now: the long-sought goal of full citizenship under the Constitution is now within our reach.
> 2. We have the power to achieve that goal: what we ourselves do will be decisive. . . .
>
> Developments at home and abroad have made it imperative that democratic rights be granted to the Negro people without further delay. A century has passed since Frederick Douglass pointed out that "the relations subsisting between the white and black people of this country is the central question of the age," and a half century since Dr. Du Bois proclaimed that "the problem of the twentieth century is the problem of the Color Line." Today we see that the prophetic truth of those statements has grown a thousandfold, and that the time has come when the question of the age and the problem of the century must be resolved.

On June 12, 1956, Paul Robeson testified in Washington, D.C., before the House Committee on Un-American Activities, which was then probing possible use of passports by communists or fellow travelers. After he got into a furious shouting session with committee members, the lawmakers cited Robeson for contempt. Robeson later told a reporter, "There was no contempt—I was just standing my ground."

was a man ahead of his time: his strong emphasis on black dignity and independence is often viewed as a forerunner of the "Black Power" movement of the late 1960s and early 1970s.

Robeson's controversial political causes and beliefs thrust him back into the national spotlight again and again. In 1952, he made national headlines when he was refused permission to cross the U.S.-Canadian border to perform for a Vancouver labor union, even though a passport was not required for U.S.-Canadian travel. Threatened with a $5,000 fine and up to five years in prison if he tried to leave the United States, Robeson decided to sing to the unionists over the telephone from Seattle. That spring, the Vancouver union and a Seattle-based union asked Robeson to perform at Peace Arch Park, on the U.S.-Canadian border. Standing on the American side, Robeson sang for an audience of some 30,000 Canadians and 5,000 Americans. The Peace Arch concert was so successful that Robeson gave one annually until 1956, when the U.S. government finally permitted him to travel to Canada. That same year, Robeson was back in the spotlight again, when the House Committee on Un-American Activities summoned him to testify. Asked why he had chosen to live in the United States rather than the USSR, Robeson defiantly replied: "Because my father was a slave, and my people died to build this country, and I am going to stay right here and have a part of it, just like you. And no fascist-minded people will drive me from it. Is that clear?"

WORLD TRAVELER ONCE MORE

In June 1958, Robeson finally regained his right to travel abroad when the U.S. Supreme Court ruled that it was unconstitutional for the State Department to revoke an American citizen's passport based on his or her beliefs or associations. Shortly after the Supreme Court ruling, Robeson held his first New York concert in more than a decade at Carnegie Hall. By the late 1950s, anti-communist feeling had diminished somewhat among the American public, and the concert was well attended and received generally positive reviews from critics.

In July 1958, Essie and Paul Robeson boarded a plane for London, where the entertainer received a warm welcome and performed at several sold-out concerts. In August, he began

On August 30, 1958, Paul Robeson *(right)* smiles as he poses with
Premier Nikita Khrushchev of the Soviet Union at the Black Sea Summer
Resort in Crimea, Russia. Robeson and his wife were then touring Europe.

a highly successful tour of the Soviet Union. The Soviet government had raised Robeson to almost heroic status during
the height of the Cold War, awarding him the International
Stalin Peace Prize in 1952 and even naming a mountain for
him. Enthusiastic crowds greeted him wherever he went. At
concerts and during televised interviews, Robeson thanked
the Soviet people repeatedly for their moral support over
the years. He and Essie were also invited by Premier Nikita
Khrushchev to visit him at his summer vacation retreat in

Yalta. Khrushchev had emerged as the USSR's top leader after Joseph Stalin's death from a cerebral hemorrhage in 1953.

Following a tour of the British Isles with Larry Brown, Robeson returned to the USSR for a two-month stay in late 1958, most of which he spent in hospitals and sanatoriums, being treated for circulatory problems and exhaustion. Although still feeling rundown, he flew to England in April 1959 to begin a six-month run of *Othello* at the Shakespeare Theatre in Stratford-upon-Avon. Throughout 1960, Robeson maintained a grueling pace. He toured the British Isles, Australia, and New Zealand with Larry Brown; made appearances and collected awards in numerous Western European cities; and paid long visits to the Soviet Union and its communist satellite, East Germany, where he was awarded the Order of the Star of International Friendship.

FINAL YEARS

Since the mid-1950s, Robeson had suffered from periodic bouts of depression and anxiety. By early 1961, his mental health had taken a turn for the worse. In March, he suddenly decided to travel alone from London to Moscow. In the early morning hours of March 27, Robeson was discovered in his Moscow hotel room with his wrists slashed. Robeson's botched suicide attempt is surrounded by mystery. His visits to the Soviet Union and other communist countries had long ago brought Robeson to the attention of the Central Intelligence Agency (CIA), a U.S. government agency founded in 1947 to conduct and coordinate intelligence activities abroad. Paul Robeson Jr. has suggested that his father's breakdown occurred after CIA operatives slipped him a powerful hallucinogenic drug at a party in his Moscow hotel room. Robeson's biographer, Martin Duberman, however, has another theory. He believes that Robeson, haunted by what had happened to his Jewish friends during Stalin's brutal purge of the 1940s, had fallen into a deep depression after several Moscow acquaintances begged for his help in getting relatives out of Soviet prisons.

Essie and Paul Jr. rushed to Moscow to be with Robeson. After being treated for several weeks at a Russian clinic, Robeson, seemingly much improved, flew back to London with his wife and son. Once in England, however, his depression quickly returned. Over the next 18 months, doctors at a London psychiatric hospital administered a series of 54 electroshock treatments to Robeson—an extraordinarily large number by today's standards. Disturbed by the massive electroconvulsive therapy his father was receiving, Paul Jr. persuaded him to transfer to an East German medical clinic for treatment in 1963.

Eslanda Robeson

Like her famous husband, Eslanda Robeson was a scholar, writer, and dedicated civil rights activist. During the 1930s, she studied anthropology, with a focus on black populations, at London University. In 1936, she took her son, Paul Jr., on a six-month tour of Africa, chronicling their experiences in her book, *African Journey*, published in 1945. Four years later, she coauthored another book, *American Argument*, with the American writer and social reformer Pearl S. Buck, in which the two women discussed their views on world peace, race relations, and politics.

Like her husband, Essie embraced the anti-fascist cause during the 1930s. She also shared his admiration for the Soviet Union and faith in socialism as the political system most likely to bring full freedom and equality to oppressed black Americans and Africans. During the 1950s, she served as the United Nations correspondent for the *New World Review*, a pro-Soviet journal. On July 7, 1953, Essie was called before the Senate Permanent Subcommittee on Investigations to testify about her alleged communist ties. She proved to be a self-assured and articulate witness. Even though she refused to answer many of her examiners' questions, asserting her Fifth Amendment rights, even the subcommittee's chairman, Senator Joseph McCarthy, had to admit that Eslanda Robeson was "a very charming woman—an intelligent lady."

In December 1963, after a four-month stay at the East Berlin clinic, Robeson told Essie that he was ready to return home to the United States. He wanted to spend more time with his grandson and granddaughter—Paul Jr.'s children with his wife, Marilyn Greenberg Robeson—and be closer to the African-American civil rights movement, which was burgeoning under the leadership of Martin Luther King Jr. For the first two years after his return to the United States, Robeson lived quietly in Harlem and continued to receive regular psychiatric care on an outpatient basis. He also spent a great deal of time in Philadelphia with his sister, Marian, a retired schoolteacher. On December 13, 1965, Essie Robeson died in a New York City hospital of breast cancer, which she had been battling for several years. Soon after, Robeson, still suffering from circulatory problems and recurrent bouts of depression, decided to move in permanently with Marian.

For the next decade, Robeson lived in nearly complete seclusion in his sister's Philadelphia home. In late December 1975, he was hospitalized for a stroke. On January 23, 1976, following a second stroke, Paul Robeson died at the age of 77. Four days later, 5,000 mourners attended a funeral service for the famed performer and activist at Mother A.M.E. Zion Church in Harlem. Robeson's ashes were interred at Ferncliff Cemetery, north of New York City. Inscribed on Robeson's simple bronze grave marker is a quotation from his June 24, 1937, speech in London protesting the fascist campaign to overthrow Spain's democratically elected government: "The artist must elect to fight for freedom or slavery. I have made my choice. I had no alternative."

"LOYALTY TO ONE'S CONVICTIONS"

From the late 1940s through the 1960s, Paul Robeson's radical political beliefs and outspoken admiration for the Soviet Union made him a virtual pariah in his home country. Finally, during the last five years of his life, Robeson began to receive

Almost 30 years after Paul Robeson died in near obscurity, his son, Paul Robeson Jr., poses next to a U.S. postage stamp honoring his father in Princeton, New Jersey, on January 20, 2004.

a series of honors from both black and white organizations. These included the Whitney Young Memorial Award from the National Urban League; an honorary doctor of law degree from his father's alma mater, Lincoln University; and an honorary doctor of the arts degree from Rutgers University (formerly Rutgers College). In 1954, during the height of the anti-communist hysteria in the United States, the Rutgers University Athletic Department had neglected to include Robeson's name on a published list of the 65 greatest football players in the school's history. In 1970, Rutgers sought to make up for this snub by nominating Robeson for the National College Football Hall of Fame. (Even though Robeson was renominated for the honor annually from 1970 on, he would not actually be inducted into the College Football Hall of Fame until 1995.)

According to his son, Robeson was particularly gratified by two honors he received in 1972. The first was being named by *Ebony* magazine as one of the 10 all-time great figures of black history, and the second was being elected as a charter member to the National Theater Hall of Fame. Robeson was also deeply moved by a salute to him at Carnegie Hall in April 1973, in honor of his seventy-fifth birthday, arranged by the black entertainer and activist Harry Belafonte. The star-studded program closed with a recorded message from Robeson: "Though I have not been able to be active for several years, I want you to know that I am the same Paul, dedicated as ever to the worldwide cause of humanity for freedom, peace, and brotherhood."

In the decades since his death, Robeson's many important contributions as an athlete, performing artist, scholar, anticolonial and labor activist, and forerunner of the American civil rights and black pride movements have been the subject of dozens of articles, books, and documentaries. More than a century after Robeson's birth, his place in American history is still being debated. Robeson was not perfect—his stubborn unwillingness to acknowledge the dark side of Soviet rule is hard to comprehend. Yet, his selfless commitment to the social causes he held dearest—equal civil rights for African Americans, political freedom for those forced to live under colonial rule, and a greater share in the wealth created by their labor for working men and women everywhere—continues to inspire. Robeson never backed down when it came to fighting for what he believed to be right, regardless of the risks to his career, his financial well-being, and even his personal safety. In *Here I Stand*, Robeson wrote that the central theme of the life of his chief role model, his father William Robeson, was "loyalty to one's convictions. Unbending. Despite anything." In his own unbending loyalty to his convictions, Paul Robeson more than lived up to his father's legacy.

1898 Paul Leroy Robeson is born on April 9 in Princeton, New Jersey.

1915–1919 Attends Rutgers College on an academic scholarship; gains national attention as one of country's top college football players.

1919 Moves to Harlem and enters law school.

1921 Marries Eslanda "Essie" Cardozo Goode.

1923 Works briefly for a New York law firm after graduating from Columbia Law School.

1924 Stars in Eugene O'Neill's *The Emperor Jones* and *All God's Chillun Got Wings*.

1925 Concert with pianist Lawrence Brown, featuring African-American music, is a resounding success.

1928 Performing career soars after appearing in London production of *Show Boat*.

1930 Takes lead role in William Shakespeare's *Othello* on the London stage.

1934 Visits the Soviet Union for the first time.

1938 Performs for Republican troops in Spain; commitment to antifascism grows.

1939 After living in London for 10 years, returns to United States upon the outbreak of World War II.

1943 Stars in *Othello* on Broadway.

1949 Speech about African Americans and the USSR creates controversy in April. Anti-Robeson riot after a concert in Peekskill, New York, in September leaves nearly 150 people injured.

1950 Passport revoked by the U.S. State Department and is not reinstated for eight years.

1961 Suffers mental breakdown during a visit to Moscow in March.

1963 Returns to the United States following five years abroad; continues treatment for variety of psychological and physical ailments.

1976 Dies in Philadelphia on January 23 after living in virtual seclusion for more than a decade.

Ehrlich, Scott. *Paul Robeson.* New York: Chelsea House, 1988.

Ford, Carin T. *Paul Robeson: "I Want to Make Freedom Ring."* Berkeley Heights, N.J.: Enslow Publishers, 2008.

Holmes, Burnham. *Paul Robeson: A Voice of Struggle.* Austin, Tex.: Raintree Steck-Vaughn, 1995.

Robeson, Paul. *Here I Stand.* Boston: Beacon Press, 1958.

Robeson, Paul, Jr. *The Undiscovered Paul Robeson: An Artist's Journey, 1898–1939.* New York: John Wiley & Sons, 2001.

———. *The Undiscovered Paul Robeson: Quest for Freedom, 1939–1976.* Hoboken, N.J.: John Wiley & Sons, 2010.

Stewart, Jeffrey C., ed. *Paul Robeson: Artist and Citizen.* Piscataway, N.J.: Rutgers University Press, 1998.

WEB SITES
Paul Robeson (Electronic New Jersey: A Digital Archive of New Jersey History)
http://www2.scc.rutgers.edu/njh/PaulRobeson/

Paul Robeson Foundation
http://www.paulrobesonfoundation.org/index.html

Paul Robeson, The Artist as Activist and Social Thinker
http://www.africawithin.com/clarke/clarke_on_robeson.htm

Paul Robeson: Voice of a Century, by Paul Robeson Jr.
http://www.black-collegian.com/issues/1998-02/probeson.shtml

page

Page numbers in *italics* indicate photos or illustrations.

About the Author

Louise Chipley Slavicek received her master's degree in history from the University of Connecticut. She is the author of numerous articles on American and world history for scholarly journals and for young people's magazines, including *Highlights for Children*, *Cobblestone*, and *Calliope*. Her more than two-dozen books for young people include *Women of the American Revolution*, *I.M. Pei*, and *The Treaty of Versailles*. She lives in Ohio with her husband, Jim, a research biologist, and their two children, Krista and Nathan.